National Park Service Comprehensive Survey of the American Public

2008–2009

Natural Resource Report NPS/NRPC/SSD/NRR—2011/295

Wyoming Survey & Analysis Center
University of Wyoming

Laramie, Wyoming

August 2011

U.S. Department of the Interior
National Park Service
Natural Resource Stewardship and Science
Fort Collins, Colorado

The National Park Service publishes a range of reports that address natural resource topics of interest and applicability to a broad audience in the National Park Service and others in natural resource management, including scientists, conservation and environmental constituencies, and the public.

The Natural Resource Report Series is used to disseminate high-priority, current natural resource management information with managerial application. The series targets a general, diverse audience, and may contain NPS policy considerations or address sensitive issues of management applicability.

All manuscripts in the series receive the appropriate level of peer review to ensure that the information is scientifically credible, technically accurate, appropriately written for the intended audience, and designed and published in a professional manner. This report received formal peer review by subject-matter experts who were not directly involved in the collection, analysis, or reporting of the data, and whose background and expertise put them on par technically and scientifically with the authors of the information.

Views, statements, findings, conclusions, recommendations, and data in this report do not necessarily reflect views and policies of the National Park Service, U.S. Department of the Interior. Mention of trade names or commercial products does not constitute endorsement or recommendation for use by the U.S. Government.

This report is available from the Social Science Division at http://www.nature.nps.gov/ socialscience/ and the Natural Resource Publications Management website at http://www.nature.nps.gov/publications/nrpm/.

Please cite this publication as:

NPS 999/106556, August 2011

Contents

Executive Summary

In 2008 and 2009 the National Park Service (NPS) conducted its second Comprehensive Survey of the American Public (CSAP2), a nationwide telephone survey consisting of 15-minute interviews with more than 4,000 respondents across the United States. Several questions contained in the first NPS comprehensive survey conducted in 2000 (CSAP1) were replicated in this second iteration. Both surveys obtained information on public attitudes and behaviors related to programs and services provided by the NPS, as well as on demographic characteristics of recent visitors and non-visitors to the National Park System. CSAP2 was designed, administered, and analyzed on behalf of the NPS by the Wyoming Survey & Analysis Center (WYSAC) at the University of Wyoming.

This technical report describes results from CSAP2 for the nation as a whole. For some questions, the report also compares responses between recent visitors and non-visitors and between residents in each of the seven NPS administrative regions. Highlights include:

1.   Almost half (47%) of American adults responding to the survey could name a valid National Park System unit they had visited during the previous two years. Using this definition of recent visitation, the District of Columbia in the NPS National Capital Region recorded the highest percentage of visitors among its residents (71%), followed by the Alaska Region (60%). The lowest percentages of recent visitors lived in the Southeast (39%) and Midwest (41%) regions. [See the detailed tabulations for question Q6c in the main report, below.]

2.   Recent visitors differed significantly from non-visitors in the type of vacation trips they preferred. Visitors more often said they liked trips to experience nature "a lot" (65% vs. 42%). Visitors also liked trips to see historical places or exhibits more than non-visitors did (51% vs. 38%). Conversely, visitors were less inclined than non-visitors to like trips to spas or resorts (27% vs. 40%). By smaller margins, recent visitors to NPS units were also less attracted to theme parks, out-of-town sporting events, cruise ships, and casinos [Q9].

3.   When recent visitors rated various experiences on their last visit to a national park unit, 68% said that viewing the sights of nature "added a lot" to their enjoyment. Other experiences adding a lot to the visit included seeing distant or unobstructed views (58%), getting away from the noise back home (57%), relaxing physically (56%), getting away from the bright lights back home (52%), and hearing the sounds of nature (50%) [Q11].

4.   Nationally, 70% of visitors reported viewing or photographing animals or plants during their most recent visit, while 60% said they had hiked or jogged at least 30 continuous minutes. Less commonly reported were water activities (20%) and snow sports (5%). Visitors living in the Pacific West (85%) or Alaska (83%) were most likely to have viewed or photographed animals and plants. The areas with the highest percentages of residents who hiked or jogged during their visit were the Pacific West Region (73%) and the Intermountain Region (65%) [Q14].

5.   On their most recent visit to any NPS site, 78% of visitors recalled viewing outdoor exhibits, 78% had read a park brochure, 73% went to a visitor center, 63% viewed indoor exhibits, and 51% talked informally with a ranger. While some of the services are not available at every NPS unit, those reported by less than half of all visitors included watching movies or videos about the site (39%), attending a ranger-led activity (35%), attending a cultural demonstration or performance (21%), and being involved with the Junior Ranger Program (4%) [Q15].

6.   When visitors who had used more than one of these services were asked which one added the most to enjoying their visit, the highest percentage chose viewing outdoor exhibits (22%), followed by attending a ranger-led activity (17%), talking informally with a ranger (13%), and going to the visitor center (12%) [Q15j].

7.   The vast majority of visitors got from their home to their most recently visited NPS unit by car, truck, or SUV (84%); however, 15% also traveled by plane on a portion of their trip [Q16]. Of those who went by car, truck, SUV, or RV, 15% used a rental vehicle during at least a part of their trip [Q16a].

8.   When asked why they did not visit more frequently, non-visitors most often said they "just don't know that much about National Park System units"; 32% of non-visitors strongly agreed with this statement, compared to only 8% of visitors. Non-visitors also strongly agreed that hotel and food costs in parks are too high (25%), that it takes too long to get to a park unit from their home (23%), and that reservations have to be made too far in advance (15%). Visitors viewed these three factors as the main constraints on their visitation, but the proportions of visitors who strongly agreed (13%, 11%, and 13%, respectively) were lower than among non-visitors [Q17].

9.   Less than 5% of both visitors and non-visitors strongly agreed that parks are unsafe places to visit, that NPS employees give poor service, or that National Park System units are unpleasant places for them to be [Q17].

10.   Respondents with children in their household were asked how much they agreed or disagreed that "my children are not interested in visiting National Park System units." Among visitors, less than 5% strongly agreed, while 70% strongly disagreed. For non-visitors there was 10% agreement and 57% disagreement with this statement [D9a].

11.   Among visitors, 6% strongly agreed that high entrance fees are a deterrent to more frequent visits; for non-visitors, the figure was 12% [Q17].

12.   In response to an open-ended question, 38% of visitors and 45% of non-visitors said that the most important thing the NPS could do to encourage them to visit more frequently would be to advertise, publicize, and provide more information. Less than 7% of both visitors and non-visitors suggested lowering entrance fees or making admission free as a way to encourage them to visit more often [Q18].

13. Members of the public can assist parks in many ways. When asked if they were aware of specific methods of assistance before the survey, 75% of visitors said they knew they could donate money to parks, and 58% of non-visitors said the same. The possibility of volunteering time also was well known, especially by visitors (62%). However, the majority of both visitors and non-visitors were unaware of opportunities to donate equipment or artifacts or to join a park's friends association [Q23]. Among those who were aware of any of these ways to help parks, most visitors (61%) and even more non-visitors (79%) reported that they had never done any of them [Q24].

14. Both visitors and non-visitors were asked about the importance of "hearing the sounds of nature" for enjoying an experience in the "wild or undeveloped areas of a large national park." About equal numbers of both groups replied that this would be very important for their enjoyment (74% of visitors and 76% of non-visitors) [Q25]. When asked about the importance of hearing "cultural and historical sounds" in parks such as Gettysburg, Valley Forge, or Mesa Verde, 56% of visitors and 60% of non-visitors said this would be very important to their enjoyment [Q27].

15. Respondents were asked their opinion of the statement that "I should be able to go to a national park and not hear mechanized sounds like engine noise and cell phones when I am in wild or undeveloped areas." Among visitors, 49% strongly agreed, as did 45% of non-visitors [Q26]. On a related question, 38% of visitors and 39% of non-visitors strongly agreed that "aircraft flights should be limited over wild and undeveloped areas" of large national parks [Q28d]. Similarly, 34% of visitors and 36% of non-visitors *disagreed* strongly that "jet-skiing and snowmobiling should be allowed in these parks" [Q28k].

16. Respondents were asked about several recreation and natural resource management issues in large parks such as Yellowstone, Grand Canyon, or Great Smoky Mountains. More than three-quarters (77%) of both visitors and non-visitors strongly agreed that such parks should be free of water pollution from outside sources [Q28g], and substantial majorities also said they should be free of externally caused air pollution (63% of visitors; 71% of non-visitors) [Q28e].

17. Both visitors (64%) and non-visitors (65%) agreed strongly that large national parks should provide basic visitor facilities, such as roads, trails, restrooms, and water fountains. However, they were less supportive of major facilities such as lodges, restaurants, and stores, with only 22% of visitors and 28% of non-visitors strongly agreeing that these should be provided [Q28].

18. Among visitors, 26% strongly agreed with the statement "plants that do not occur naturally in these parks should be removed," while 12% strongly disagreed. Non-visitors were sharply divided on this issue: 23% strongly supported removal, but an almost identical proportion strongly opposed it [Q28a].

19.   A similar division is evident on a question about removing non-native animals: 18% of visitors strongly agreed with removal of animals that do not occur naturally in the parks and 15% disagreed. Among non-visitors, 25% strongly favored removal, with 22% strongly against this [Q28b].

20.   A majority of both visitors (54%) and non-visitors (58%) strongly endorsed the statement "animals that used to occur naturally in these parks should be brought back." Less than 8% of either group expressed strong disagreement [Q28c].

Detailed results on all of the questions in CSAP2 are provided in the tables of this national report and in separate regional reports. The main report that follows begins with an explanation of the survey methods.

In addition to this National Technical Report, the following companion reports will also be published.

- Racial and Ethnic Diversity of National Park System Visitors and Non-Visitors

- Broad Comparisons to the 2000 Survey

- Parks as Preferred Vacation Destinations

- Opinions on Park Management Issues

- Soundscapes Report

- Regional Reports (seven)

- Non-Response Bias Report

Authors

Patricia A. Taylor, Ph.D., Professor and WYSAC Faculty Affiliate
Burke D. Grandjean, Ph.D., Professor and WYSAC Executive Director
Bistra Anatchkova, Ph.D., WYSAC Survey Research Manager

With the assistance of Brian Harnisch, WYSAC Assistant Research Scientist, and other WYSAC staff

Wyoming Survey & Analysis Center
University of Wyoming • Dept. 3925
1000 East University Avenue • Laramie, WY 82071
wysac@uwyo.edu • http://wysac.uwyo.edu
(307) 766-2189 • Fax: (307) 766-2759

Patricia A. Taylor, the Principal Investigator on the NPS Comprehensive Survey, is Professor of Sociology and a Faculty Affiliate of the Wyoming Survey & Analysis Center (WYSAC) at the University of Wyoming. Her recent research includes national surveys for the Departments of the Interior and Agriculture and for the Environmental Protection Agency, as well as several park-specific projects.

Burke D. Grandjean is the Executive Director of the Wyoming Survey & Analysis Center and a Professor of Statistics and Sociology at the University of Wyoming. He served as Co-Principal Investigator on the NPS Comprehensive Survey.

Bistra Anatchkova is Manager of WYSAC's Survey Research Center and Co-Principal Investigator on the NPS Comprehensive Survey. With more than two decades of experience in survey methodology, she has overseen previous national surveys conducted by telephone, mail, and on the Internet.

WYSAC has a staff of 20 full-time employees and numerous part-time student workers, research aides, and interviewers. Together they conduct public opinion surveys, evaluation research, and software development for state and local governments and federal agencies.

Acknowledgments

The WYSAC research team is very grateful to James Gramann, Ph.D., Professor of Recreation, Park and Tourism Sciences at Texas A&M University and Visiting Social Scientist of the National Park Service. His assistance was of immense value throughout the current project, from its initial conception and design through the peer review and final editing of this report.

The researchers also thank Fred Solop and the staff of the former Social Research Laboratory at Northern Arizona University for assistance with the 2000 data; John Dennis and Darryll Johnson of the National Park Service for their input designing the 2008–2009 survey instrument; Sharon Lohr of Arizona State University for consultations on the sampling plan; the anonymous reviewers of this and other reports on the project for their careful, detailed, and helpful comments; and Diane Breeding of Texas A&M University for essential administrative support during all phases of the project.

Introduction

This is the national technical report of the 2008–2009 National Park Service (NPS) Comprehensive Survey of the American Public. Although the NPS obtains opinion data from visitors in several ways, the comprehensive survey is unique because it is the only national survey conducted for the NPS that interviews both visitors and non-visitors to the National Park System.

The first NPS Comprehensive Survey of the American Public (CSAP1) was conducted in 2000 by Northern Arizona University. It generated a series of reports now archived on the NPS Social Science Division website at http://www.nature.nps.gov/socialscience/.

In 2009, the Wyoming Survey & Analysis Center (WYSAC) at the University of Wyoming completed the second iteration of the comprehensive survey (CSAP2). Like the previous survey, CSAP2 was conducted by telephone interview on a nationwide sample. The second survey sought to provide updated information on some of the questions asked in the 2000 survey, while also addressing additional topics and refining the survey methods.

The present report tabulates the national-level results for each item in the CSAP2 questionnaire and provides technical details on the methods. Tables are also reported comparing recent NPS visitors to non-visitors and showing breakdowns across the seven NPS administrative regions.

In addition, seven separate regional reports have been produced for distribution on the NPS website referenced above. A series of topical reports is also available separately that examine differences across major racial and ethnic groups, compare results over time between CSAP1 and CSAP2, and address other methodological and substantive issues.

Survey Methods

Both CSAP1 and CSAP2 were designed to represent not only the opinions of the U.S. population as a whole (adults in the 50 states and the District of Columbia), but also those of residents in each of the seven NPS regions. As in 2000, the U.S. territories of American Samoa, Guam, the Northern Mariana Islands, the U.S. Virgin Islands, and the Commonwealth of Puerto Rico were excluded from the sample. To maintain comparability with CSAP1, the regional calling areas departed slightly from the administrative boundaries used by the NPS, since telephone area codes and regional boundaries do not coincide. For purposes of the survey, the National Capital Region calling area included only the District of Columbia (area code 202), although this region also administers some parks in Virginia, Maryland, and West Virginia. For example, Theodore Roosevelt Island (in the Potomac River) is administered by the National Capital Region (NCR), but the park lies within the state of Virginia. Harpers Ferry National Historical Park in West Virginia also is administered by the NCR, as is Antietam National Battlefield in Maryland. As was done in CSAP1, households in these latter states were included in the calling area for the Northeast Region.

The seven calling areas were as follows:

- Alaska Region (AKR) – the state of Alaska;

- Intermountain Region (IMR) – states of Arizona, Colorado, Montana, New Mexico, Oklahoma, Texas, Utah, and Wyoming;

- Midwest Region (MWR) – states of Arkansas, Illinois, Indiana, Iowa, Kansas, Michigan, Minnesota, Missouri, Nebraska, North Dakota, Ohio, South Dakota, and Wisconsin;

- National Capital Region (NCR) – District of Columbia;

- Northeast Region (NER) – states of Connecticut, Delaware, Maine, Maryland, Massachusetts, New Hampshire, New Jersey, New York, Pennsylvania, Rhode Island, Vermont, Virginia, and West Virginia;

- Pacific West Region (PWR) – states of California, Hawaii, Idaho, Nevada, Oregon, and Washington;

- Southeast Region (SER) – states of Alabama, Florida, Georgia, Kentucky, Louisiana, Mississippi, North Carolina, South Carolina, and Tennessee.

In tables presenting regional data, the regions are displayed from west to east (which also generally reflects the percentage of park lands in each region from highest to lowest).

Sampling Issues

The data for this study were developed from a national sample of residential landline telephone numbers and cell phones. The sample was obtained from an established vendor of sampling services (Marketing Systems Group) and was generated using Random Digit Dialing methods (RDD).

Landline and Cell Phone Samples

In planning the sample, a number of issues had to be considered. First, because of the rapid increase in cell-only and cell-reliant households throughout the U.S., a sample of landline telephones can no longer be taken as representing the population (Brick *et al.*, 2007; Keeter *et al.*, 2007). Therefore, a separate sample of cell phone numbers (randomly generated from the known area codes and telephone prefixes dedicated to cell phones) supplemented the primary landline sample. Cell phones were not included in the CSAP1 sample.

Regional Subsamples

Second, as in the 2000 survey, the landline sample was disproportionately stratified to produce approximately 500 completed interviews from residents in each of the seven NPS regions. The survey ultimately generated 3,550 completed landline interviews, spread almost evenly across the regions.

The cell sample was not pre-stratified by region. Cell phone users are, on average, more mobile than the general population, and the area code in which a cell phone was issued may not represent the area code where the individual resides.[1] For this study, the portion of the sample from cell phone numbers produced an additional 553 completed interviews nationwide.

Landline respondents initially were assigned to a region based on their telephone area code. However, a few landline respondents reported living in a different state from that indicated by area codes. During analysis, respondents in both the cell phone and landline samples were assigned to NPS regions based on their answers to a question about their state of residence (asked in the introductory section of the questionnaire). In the final tally of 4,103 landline and cell interviews, the regional totals ranged from 492 in the National Capital Region (D.C.) to 622 in the Northeast Region, as shown in the following table.

Number of Respondents Nationally by NPS Region

National	AKR	PWR	IMR	MWR	SER	NER	NCR
4,103	548	603	614	611	613	622	492

---

[1] A dilemma for future surveys is that as cell phone users age (and, say, get out of college or change jobs) they are more likely to move and take their cell phone numbers with them, not wishing to lose contact with family and friends. Therefore, with cell phone usage spreading, more individuals have cell phone area codes unrelated to the landline area codes where they reside. Yet without regional stratification, a national sample yields few cell phone cases in the smallest NPS regions (AKR and NCR). This will be an important issue for CSAP3.

Within-household Respondent Selection
A third sampling issue involved converting the sample of landline telephone households into a representative sample of individual adults. This required selecting one adult (18 years of age or older) to complete the interview from each household contacted.

The landline sample was randomly divided into thirds, and three separate selection techniques were used to sample within households. First, to replicate the approach used in CSAP1, interviewers asked to speak to the adult in the household who had had the *most recent* birthday. This "last birthday" approach is a commonly used, quasi-random method of respondent selection that has been shown to give acceptably representative results as long as the target population does not include children (Grandjean *et al.*, 2004).

To counter-balance against possible bias in that method, a "next birthday" approach and simple random selection also were used. In a random one-third of the landline sample, the interviewers asked to speak with the adult who would have the *next* birthday. In the remaining third of the landline sample, the interviewer asked to speak to a specified respondent who was selected by computer using a random-number generator (e.g., "the second-oldest adult" in the household). Households with only one adult member did not require within-household selection in the landline sample. The cell phone sample also required no additional selection, under the assumption that a cell phone is used primarily by one person and generates a sample of individuals, rather than a sample of households.

Statistical checks on these three methods of respondent selection indicate that the method of selection for CSAP1 did not bias results, and that all three methods used in CSAP2 yield comparable results. Method of respondent selection is significantly related to only one of 33 variables examined in these checks, which is about what would be expected by chance alone.

Seasonal Variations
In CSAP1, all interviewing was completed in a 90-day period between February 21 and May 21, 2000. Because visitation and activities at NPS units vary seasonally, CSAP2 spread the interviewing across all four seasons of the year. Interviewing began with the spring season on April 10, 2008. By the end of that season's interviewing on June 20, the first 1,013 completions had been obtained. An additional 714 interviews were completed during the summer (through September 21), and another 1,228 in the fall (through December 23). The remaining 1,148 winter completions were obtained between January 5 and March 18, 2009. Checks comparing results from the 2000 survey to the 2008–2009 results found no substantial seasonal differences in the questions analyzed.

Spanish-language Interviews
A final sampling issue concerned the language of the questionnaire. The interviews for CSAP1 occurred exclusively in English. This restricted the sample in 2000 to respondents who could converse in that language. For CSAP2, the sample included respondents who could converse either in English or in Spanish (although it still omitted those who exclusively used or preferred any other language). Households that were identified in the initial calling as potentially requiring a Spanish-speaking interviewer were called back by bilingual interviewers to seek participation. During that follow-up calling, the interviewers had immediate access (using software for Computer Aided Telephone Interviewing) to both English and Spanish versions of the

questionnaire, and they used whichever was more comfortable for the respondent. A total of 807 numbers were called back by bilingual interviewers, and 96 respondents were actually interviewed in Spanish, including nine interviews conducted in a mixture of Spanish and English.

Weighting the Sample

Post-stratification
The methods used for weighting the respondent data for CSAP1 and CSAP2 were not identical, but they were closely similar. In both surveys, two different sets of weights were used, one set for regional comparisons and another for national estimates. The landline portion of the sample was stratified by the seven NPS regions, with the least populous regions (AKR and NCR) being over-sampled to obtain enough completed interviews for statistical analysis of that region's residents. Therefore, to provide analysis at the national level, the nationwide results had to be weighted according to the proportion of the adult population in each of the seven regions.

In CSAP2, the landline sample was first weighted to account for the number of adults in the household and the number of landline telephones; then the combined landline/cell sample was weighted to reflect cell phone usage (as estimated by the National Center for Health Statistics). Weights initially were derived separately for each region, and iteratively adjusted to bring the sample data into correspondence with independent regional population distributions on age, gender, ethnicity, and race (using benchmarks obtained from the Census Bureau's Population Estimates Program). Then the regional subsamples were pooled, re-weighted to reflect the national population distribution across regions, and again adjusted iteratively to correspond with national distributions on the demographic variables. CSAP1 used the same demographics for post-stratification weighting, but did not account for cell phone usage.

Deflating the Sample Size
Unlike CSAP1, in CSAP2 the weights were deflated to reduce the weighted sample sizes by about one-third. The appropriate deflation factors were calculated nationally and separately for each region so as to compensate for an increase in the statistical margin of error that is produced by weighting survey data (Dorofeev and Grant, 2006). Correcting the margin of error for the weighting is useful when testing for statistically significant differences. For descriptive statistics such as percentages, results are unaffected by deflating the sample sizes. CSAP1 did not provide significance tests in its reports, and did not deflate the sample size.

Survey Participation

Completion Rates
Survey participation rates may be assessed in various ways. A "completion rate" can be defined as the number of completed interviews divided by the number of respondents who progressed past the introductory screening questions. So defined, the completion rate for CSAP2 was 91% nationally, with a range by region of 90% to 93%. In other words, all but 9% of selected respondents who started the main part of the survey completed it. CSAP1 reported a completion rate of 88% nationally and rates by region that ranged from 73% to 95%.

Response Rates

A completion rate generally considers only households that were successfully contacted, whereas a "response rate" includes in its denominator all eligible phone numbers in the sample, even if no one ever answered. Response rates, calculated by any of several accepted formulas, often yield much lower numerical values than completion rates. The overall response rate for CSAP2 was 12.5% (using the "RR3" formula defined by the American Association for Public Opinion Research). For landlines the response rate was 15.4%, while for cell phones it was 5.7%.[2]

Potential Self-selection

The CSAP1 survey conducted in 2000 did not report a response rate, so a direct comparison of response rates between the two studies cannot be made. However, because response rates to telephone surveys generally have been dropping over the past decade, CSAP1 may have had a higher rate of response than CSAP2. In turn, it may be that the effect of self-selection of survey respondents with an interest in national parks was greater for CSAP2 than for CSAP1. For example, people who were recent or regular visitors to the parks could have been more interested in the topic of the survey, and hence more likely to agree to participate. This kind of self-selection could impact several measures drawn from the survey data, including the percentage of households reporting a recent visit to an NPS unit.

To mitigate potential problems from non-response, survey procedures routinely involve weighting the survey results. As discussed above, weighting is a statistical adjustment that brings selected demographic characteristics of the survey sample in line with independent measures of the same demographic characteristics, such as those reported by the U.S. Bureau of the Census. To the degree that demographic factors used in the weighting are correlated with other characteristics addressed in the survey, such as opinions and behavior, weighting helps to reduce the adverse effects of non-response. However, as was also acknowledged in the CSAP1 report, some bias in the estimates is unavoidable when missed people have characteristics different from those of interviewed people in the same demographic group.

---

[2] In part, the lower rate for cell phones reflects limitations on when callers are permitted to interview cell phone users. For example, cell phone interviews cannot be conducted if the respondent is driving. Also, time on a cell phone for an interview may count against the respondent's allotted monthly minutes, producing more refusals.

Identifying Recent Visitors and Non-visitors

An important set of innovations introduced in CSAP2 involved the way visitors and non-visitors were identified in a short telephone interview. For consistency with the definition used for CSAP1, "recent visitors" were defined as respondents who could name a unit of the National Park System they had visited in the previous two years. The CSAP2 interview protocols added several features to the visitation questions, designed to assist interviewers in accurately recording the names of the NPS units that respondents said they had visited most recently.

Extensive pretesting of CSAP2 revealed that direct coding of visitation status by interviewers based on respondents' reports was not always reliable. With an impatient respondent on the phone, and a list of nearly 400 units to consult, interviewers could overlook a valid but unfamiliar unit name. Furthermore, specific recall of an official park name was a very difficult cognitive task for some respondents. From preliminary focus groups and national pretest interviewing, it was clear that respondents often remembered the NPS unit they had visited not by its official name, but by its location, a colloquial alias, or some key geographic, cultural, or natural feature.

These issues were addressed in several ways. For CSAP2, a new list of NPS units was developed that included not only the official unit names, but also many commonly used aliases (for example, "Gateway Arch" and "St. Louis Arch," as well as Jefferson National Expansion Memorial; "Mount McKinley" as well as Denali National Park and Preserve). The list was organized in two ways: alphabetically by unit name or alias, and alphabetically by the state or states in which the unit was located. To simplify capturing the most likely responses, an abbreviated list of high-visitation parks was automatically displayed as part of the Computer Aided Telephone Interviewing. The full list was available to interviewers in hardcopy and as a searchable spreadsheet that they could display on their computer screens at any point during an interview. Interviewers chose whichever format for the full list they personally found more efficient.

In a further refinement, several probes were introduced in the interview script for optional use by the interviewers when they could not readily find a named unit on the list. These probes (for the unit's state, any alternative names, and its spelling) gave interviewers the information and the time they needed to search the cross-referenced list of unit names. Finally, if no valid NPS unit had yet been identified, the respondent was prompted with the names of two units in the area. If the site described by the respondent still could not be found on the list, the answer was taken down verbatim as an open-ended response.

As nearly as possible, the definition of visitor status used in this report parallels the original method employed in CSAP1. It is not a strict replication of that method, due mainly to the improvements just described in the list of NPS units. Under this definition, "visitors" include only those respondents who could name, with probes but no prompts from the interviewer, a listed unit of the National Park System that they had visited in the preceding two years.

Developing the 2008–2009 Questionnaire

The NPS conducted its first Comprehensive Survey of the American Public in 2000, and therefore had already developed an entire questionnaire with scales and response categories before the current project got under way in 2006. However, important differences existed in the issues the NPS wished to explore in CSAP2. In the fall of 2006 WYSAC personnel met in Washington, D.C., with NPS staff and a technical advisory group (social scientists from the NPS, academia, and the travel industry) to develop a draft questionnaire reflecting these new issues. In addition, WYSAC invited and received comments from several stakeholder groups, such as the National Park Hospitality Association, as part of a public commenting process required by the Paperwork Reduction Act.

In February 2007, a focus group of self-identified African Americans was held in Denver, Colorado, to evaluate the draft questionnaire for possible wording problems and misinterpretation of questions. In summer 2007, after further consultations between the NPS and WYSAC, a revised draft was translated into Spanish and then checked through back-translation by a second bilingual translator. In October 2007, a second focus group attended by persons of Hispanic descent reviewed both the English and Spanish versions. Feedback from the two focus groups on content, wording, and flow contributed to a subsequent revision of the interview form, again through a cooperative effort of the NPS and WYSAC.

Following the focus groups, WYSAC conducted cognitive interviews (Willis, 2005) on a small national landline sample. Specially trained interviewers used a modified version of the instrument to obtain feedback by telephone from 28 respondents around the country. The modified questionnaire concentrated on items new to the 2008–2009 instrument, with specific probes and follow-up questions to assess understanding and interpretation of those items. Results of the cognitive interviewing led to additional refinements in the wording and response choices for several questions.

As a final pretest, the full questionnaire was programmed for Computer Aided Telephone Interviewing, and 89 interviews were conducted on a national landline sample in March 2008. As a result of this final pretest, the NPS deleted some items to reduce the length of the interview. In addition, the NPS identified several groups of questions that would be asked of only a random half of the respondents (see "Split-ballot Design," below). This strategy maximized the number of questions that could be included in a short telephone interview without compromising the representativeness of the sample. However, sample sizes for these questions were lower (since they were asked of only half of the respondents). Results for these items are therefore reported here only at the national level, without regional breakdowns.

Interpreting the Tables

The remainder of this report provides the complete telephone interview script for CSAP2, along with tables describing the basic results. Presentation of the script begins with its introductory section, covering consent to participate, identifying eligible respondents, and addressing other methodological issues. Detailed tables are not included for that section of the questionnaire. Then all survey items from the main body of the questionnaire are presented verbatim and in the order they were asked in the interview.

A **bold** font in the script denotes wording that the telephone interviewers were required to read. Text that is not bolded indicates supplemental information that the interviewers could use, in whole or in part, at their option. Clarifications for the reader that follow some questions in the script are bracketed and prefaced with "Note to the reader." Items are numbered for ease of reference, but numbers were not visible to the interviewers and were not presented to the respondents.

Each item is accompanied by a frequency table showing the unweighted counts and percentages, as well as percentages weighted to represent the population of U.S. adults. Where relevant, tables are presented comparing recent NPS visitors to non-visitors. Many of the questions are accompanied by geographic cross-tabulations, weighted to represent the population of adults within each of the seven NPS regions. No geographic breakdowns are presented for items that, by design, were asked of only half of the respondents or less.

Beyond regional comparisons and comparisons of recent visitors with non-visitors, the data presented in this national report are not subjected here to further examination, such as comparisons across ethnic groups. A series of topical reports addressing selected issues in greater depth is scheduled for release by the NPS in 2011 and 2012. For the researcher or manager who wishes to investigate any questions further, the data set for CSAP2 is available from the Social Science Division of the NPS in an electronic format that can be read using a number of statistical software packages.

Interpreting Weighted Percents
In general, when reading tables displaying national data and showing both unweighted and weighted percentages, readers should focus on the "Weighted Percent" column. That column makes the appropriate adjustments for disproportionate sampling across the seven regions and deflates the sample size to account for the statistical impact of the weighting.

Interpreting Visitor Status
Where applicable, the frequency table is followed by a weighted cross-tabulation of that item against visitation status. In these tables, recent "visitors" are defined as adult respondents residing in the U.S. who named any National Park System site they had visited in the past two years that could be confirmed by the interviewers from a cross-indexed list as a valid unit of the system. Park sites were defined as the 391 units that officially comprised the National Park System at the time of the survey. This excluded affiliated units, national landmarks, most trails and rivers, national heritage areas, and other types of sites that the NPS helps protect, but which are not included in the National Park System.

Although the term "non-visitor" is used in the tables for persons who did not fit this specific definition of a recent visitor, that label does not mean the respondents so classified had never visited a unit of the National Park System. In fact, almost 89% of all respondents reported at least one visit in their lifetime.

Interpreting Regional Status

The regional categories in the tables denote each respondent's self-reported place of residence. As noted previously, to maintain consistency with CSAP1, the National Capital Region only includes households in the District of Columbia proper. Responses from residents of Maryland, Virginia, and West Virginia are included in the Northeast Region sample, although a small number of NCR parks are located in those states.

Because region is based on place of residence, the regional breakdowns do not signify the location of parks that respondents may have visited. When respondents answered questions about their most recent trip to a National Park System unit, the park could be in or near their home state, or in another NPS region entirely. CSAP2 is not designed for estimating characteristics of the visitor population for any single park, for all the parks in a region, or even (because international visitors are not included in the sample) for all parks nationwide.

Interpreting Statistical Test Results (p-values)

In any statistical survey, it can be useful to assess whether a difference observed in the sample also exists in the population the sample represents. In this report, chi-square tests are used to compare visitors with non-visitors and to compare responses across the seven NPS regions. The results are reported directly beneath each table. A small "p-value" on a chi-square test, such as $p < .05$ (or smaller), indicates that the difference being tested can be generalized with 95% confidence (or more) from a sample of this size to the population as a whole. In other words, the difference is statistically significant by conventional standards. A large p-value (for example, $p > .2$) suggests that the difference might well be due to chance variation in the sample and should not be considered significant in a statistical sense. Tests that are non-significant by the conventional criterion (i.e., whenever $p \geq .05$) are reported in *italics*.

Question Rotations

Split-ballot Design

To keep the questionnaire to a reasonable time limit for a telephone interview, several groups of questions were rotated so that only a random half of the sample answered some of the questions. Where this split-ballot approach was used, questions are marked in the script by notations such as "[For random subset A]."

Each of the two random subsets contained about 2,000 respondents. However, some of the questions in a rotation were asked only of visitors, reducing the sample size to about 1,000. When either of the random subsets of respondents is further divided among the seven NPS regions, the number in a region drops below 200 on some items. And when the sample is deflated to reflect the weighting, the effective sample size within a region is smaller still, producing a correspondingly wider statistical margin of error. To avoid placing undue emphasis

14

on such comparisons, regional breakdowns are not presented on the rotated questions in this national report. Separate regional reports provide descriptive results on all questions for each NPS region.

Randomized Lists

Some questions asked respondents to rate their agreement with a list of items. For all but the shortest lists, the Computer Aided Telephone Interviewing program randomized the order in which items were asked so that they were presented to respondents in varying sequences. This avoided potential bias caused by respondent fatigue or other order effects. In the interview script, these questions are marked by the notation, "[In random order]."

Interview Script, with Tables of Responses[3]

i1. **Hello, I'm calling from the University of Wyoming for a survey about recreation, and I'm NOT selling anything. First, I'm required to ask if I have I reached you on a cell phone.**

i1a. [If NOT CELL on item i1] **Your phone number was randomly chosen for a nation-wide survey. The purpose is to help the National Park Service improve its services to you and people like you. My name is** [First Name] **and I only need about 15 minutes to ask you some important questions about our national parks and historic sites. Would you be able to help me out with this?**

(As needed: It's really important that we get opinions from all types of households, whether you know much about national parks or not. The University of Wyoming is conducting this study for the National Park Service, which will use the results to better serve the public. The U.S. Office of Management and Budget has approved this research under the Paperwork Reduction Act. All of your answers are completely voluntary. Responses to this study will be used only for statistical purposes. The reports prepared will summarize findings across the sample and will not associate responses with a specific individual. We will not provide information that identifies you to anyone outside the study team, except as required by law. The National Park Service wants input from the American people about managing parks. No action may be taken against you for refusing to supply the information requested. No personal data will be recorded that will identify you. Your phone number will be separated from your answers, so the final data will be anonymous. Participation in this survey is expected to average about 15 minutes per household. U.S. Code 16-1a-7 authorizes collection of this information. The OMB approval number is 1024-0254, with an expiration date of October 31, 2010. You may direct comments on any aspect of this survey toll-free to the University of Wyoming at 1-866-966-2715.)

i1b. [If CELL to item i1] **I'm not allowed to interview you if you're driving or doing anything that could be dangerous, and I don't want to use your minutes. Is it safe to talk, or should I call back some other time?** [If Not Safe, quickly and politely end call.]

i1c. [If No (REFUSE) to item i1a] **You might only qualify for a few questions. Can I ask those, and we can stop whenever you want?** [If No, seek a callback appointment and politely end call.]

i1d. [If Yes (ACCEPT) to item i1a, i1b, or i1c] **Are you at least 18 years old?**

i1e. [If No or refuses item i1d]: **I'm sorry, but I'm not allowed to interview anyone under 18. Is there someone at this phone number who is 18 or older that I can speak to now, or could**

---

[3] Questions i1 through i4e are introductory screening questions to obtain consent, identify eligible respondents, and accomplish other methodological requirements. Except for item i2d, response frequencies are not tabulated in this report for screening questions.

I call back some other time? [If an adult comes to the phone, repeat introductory information from item i1a; if not, seek a callback appointment and politely end call.]

i1f. [If NOT CELL on item i1] **And have I reached you at a private household in the United States?** [If No, politely end call and code as ineligible.]

(As needed: Private household means a residence where one or more individuals or families live. It could be a house, an apartment, or a mobile home, but not a business or government office where nobody lives. Retirement communities, boarding houses, or other group quarters are not considered a private household unless this phone number rings directly into the living quarters of a particular individual or family, rather than ringing into a central switchboard or a phone shared with other residents.)

i1g. [If Yes to item i1f] **And do you currently live in the United States?** [If No, politely end call and code as ineligible.]

i1h. [If Yes to item i1f or i1g] **In what state do you currently live, or is it D.C.?**

i2a. [If Yes to item i1)] **In the household where you live, is there at least one residential landline phone that can be answered by a person, or does your household only have cell phones?**

(As needed: A landline phone that is only used for business, or only for a computer or fax machine, is NOT considered a residential phone. A voice-over-Internet phone, on computer, IS considered a landline.)

i2b. [If Yes to item i1] **Your cell phone number was randomly chosen for a nationwide survey. The purpose is to help the National Park Service improve its services to you and people like you. My name is** [First Name] **and I only need about 15 minutes to ask you some important questions about our national parks and historic sites.**

(As needed: [same as on item i1a].)

i2c. **In the past TWELVE MONTHS, has any member of your household visited a national park, national historic or cultural site, or national monument?**

i2d. **We'd like to know how satisfied you are with the way the National Park Service manages the national parks, national historic and cultural sites, and national monuments. In general, are you very satisfied, somewhat satisfied, neither satisfied nor dissatisfied, somewhat dissatisfied, or very dissatisfied?**

[Note to the reader: Questions i2c and i2d were included in the screening section to obtain information about households that might not complete the full interview. See the end of this section for a table of responses to item i2d.]

i3. **Including yourself, how many people age 18 or older currently live in your household?**

i4. [If Two or more on item i3 and not in cell phone sample] **To be sure our survey covers a good sampling of U.S. adults, my computer will randomly select one person in your household for me to complete the rest of the interview.**

i4a. [If selection method 1] **I need to talk to the adult in your household, age 18 or older, who had the MOST RECENT birthday. Would that be you or someone else?**

i4b. [If selection method 2] **I need to talk to the adult in your household, age 18 or older, who will have the NEXT birthday. Would that be you or someone else?**

i4c. [If selection method 3] **I need to talk to the member of your household, age 18 or older, who is the** [randomly chosen respondent; e.g., "second oldest adult"]. **Would that be you or someone else?**

i4d. [If Someone Else to item i4a, i4b, or i4c] **May I please speak to the member of your household who is the** [selected respondent]? [If someone else comes to the phone, repeat introductory information from item i1a; if not, seek a callback appointment and politely end call.]

i4e. **I also need to tell you that this interview may be monitored by my supervisor for quality assurance.**

[Note to the reader: This concludes the introductory screening questions.

Because most of these items were asked before the within-household selection of a specific adult respondent, the weights derived for the final sample of individual adults are not appropriate for use with the screening questions. For informational purposes the unweighted frequencies for Question i2d are provided immediately below.]

i2d. **We'd like to know how satisfied you are with the way the National Park Service manages the national parks, national historic and cultural sites, and national monuments. In general, are you very satisfied, somewhat satisfied, neither satisfied nor dissatisfied, somewhat dissatisfied, or very dissatisfied?**

Table Q2d. Frequency Distribution (national data, unweighted sample)

Response	Unweighted Frequency	Unweighted Percent	Cumulative Percent
Very satisfied	1,831	44.6%	44.6%
Somewhat satisfied	1,322	32.2%	76.8%
Neither satisfied nor dissatisfied	732	17.8%	94.7%
Somewhat dissatisfied	134	3.3%	98.0%
Very dissatisfied	62	1.5%	99.5%
(No answer/Refused)	22	0.5%	100.0%
Total N	4,103	100.0%	

Q5. The National Park System consists of all the units managed by the National Park Service, including national parks, historic and cultural sites, and national monuments. How many times in the past two years have you visited a unit of the National Park System?

(As needed: I have a list that we can check in a second. But for right now, I just need you to tell me how many times you THINK you personally have visited ANY of these public lands in the past two years.)

Table Q5.1. Frequency Distribution (national data, general public)

Response	Unweighted Frequency	Unweighted Percent	Weighted Percent
0 visits	1,330	33.3%	38.6%
1 visit	557	13.9%	15.6%
2 visits	567	14.2%	14.9%
3 visits	373	9.3%	8.2%
4 visits	292	7.3%	6.5%
5 visits	185	4.6%	4.2%
6 visits	141	3.5%	2.9%
7 visits	30	0.8%	0.8%
8 visits	41	1.0%	1.1%
9 visits	2	0.1%	0.0%
10 visits	121	3.0%	2.0%
11 or more visits	357	8.9%	5.2%
Total valid	3,996	100.0%	100.0%
Don't know/Not sure	90		
No answer/Refused	17		
Total missing	107		
Total N	4,103	3,996	2,637

Table Q5.2. Cross-tabulation by Region (weighted regional data, general public)

Response	AKR	PWR	IMR	MWR	SER	NER	NCR
0 visits	27.7%	32.4%	34.0%	44.0%	45.9%	37.7%	14.1%
1 visit	11.9%	16.4%	14.9%	16.1%	15.6%	15.2%	8.3%
2 visits	12.6%	16.2%	15.4%	15.5%	12.2%	13.7%	9.6%
3 visits	9.9%	8.8%	11.5%	7.0%	6.7%	7.5%	9.2%
4 visits	8.1%	7.7%	6.2%	5.8%	5.8%	7.2%	7.7%
5 visits	5.2%	4.7%	4.8%	3.1%	3.7%	4.1%	8.6%
6 visits	4.9%	3.6%	2.2%	2.2%	2.5%	3.9%	3.5%
7 visits	1.2%	1.9%	0.6%	0.3%	0.2%	1.0%	1.2%
8 visits	1.3%	--	1.4%	1.6%	0.9%	1.3%	1.1%
9 visits	--	--	--	0.2%	--	--	0.3%
10 visits	4.8%	1.6%	2.9%	0.7%	2.1%	2.4%	8.3%
11 or more visits	12.3%	6.5%	6.1%	3.6%	4.6%	6.0%	28.0%
Total	100.0%	100.0%	100.0%	100.0%	100.0%	100.0%	100.0%
Valid weighted N	356	364	409	450	386	414	275

Chi-square test: p<.001

[Note to the reader: Q5 was asked of all respondents to identify the pool of potential recent visitors, subject to later confirmation.]

Q6a. [If zero on item Q5, i.e., asked only of respondents who reported no visits within the past 2 years] **Have you ever, in your lifetime, visited a national park, historic or cultural site, monument, or other unit managed by the National Park Service?**

(As needed: I have a list that we can check in a second. But for right now, I just need you to tell me if you THINK you have ever visited any of these public lands.)

Table Q6a.1. Frequency Distribution (national data, general public)

Response	Unweighted Frequency	Unweighted Percent	Weighted Percent
(One or more visits on Q5)	2,666	65.6%	60.8%
Yes (ever visited)	1,073	26.4%	27.9%
No	322	7.9%	11.3%
Total valid	4,061	100.0%	100.0%
(Don't know/Not sure)	41		
(No Answer/Refused)	1		
Total missing	42		
Total N	4,103	4,061	2,665

Table Q6a.2. Cross-tabulation by Region (weighted regional data, general public)

Response	AKR	PWR	IMR	MWR	SER	NER	NCR
(One or more on Q5)	71.5%	65.9%	65.0%	55.2%	54.6%	61.0%	83.3%
Yes (ever visited)	19.5%	26.1%	26.3%	33.1%	27.3%	28.4%	13.0%
No	8.9%	8.0%	8.8%	11.7%	18.1%	10.6%	3.7%
Total	100.0%	100.0%	100.0%	100.0%	100.0%	100.0%	100.0%
Valid weighted N	359	374	414	456	381	422	282

Chi-square test: p<.001

21

Q6b. [If Yes to item Q6a, i.e., asked of respondents who reported no visits within the past two years but said they had visited in their lifetime] **We want to ask about the last time you visited a unit of the National Park System. Was your most recent visit ...**

(Read ONLY responses [in bold], but code [never or within two years] if volunteered. As needed: The National Park System includes national parks, national historic and cultural sites, and national monuments. I have a list of the 391[4] units, so we can check in a second. But for right now, I just need you to tell me how long ago you THINK you last visited ANY of these public lands.)

Table Q6b.1. Frequency Distribution (national data, general public)

Response	Unweighted Frequency	Unweighted Percent	Weighted Percent
(Never visited on Q6a)	322	8.0%	11.4%
More than 5 years ago	709	17.5%	18.7%
From 2 to 5 years ago	329	8.1%	8.5%
(Volunteered: Within 2 years)	20	0.5%	0.5%
(One or more visits on Q5)	2,666	65.9%	61.0%
Total valid	4,046	100.0%	100.0%
(Don't know/Not sure)	14		
(No Answer/Refused)	1		
(Missing on Q6a)	42		
Total missing	57		
Total N	4,103	4,046	2,657

Table Q6b.2. Cross-tabulation by Region (weighted regional data, general public)

Response	AKR	PWR	IMR	MWR	SER	NER	NCR
(Never visited on Q6a)	9.0%	8.0%	8.8%	11.7%	18.2%	10.7%	3.7%
More than 5 years ago	13.3%	17.6%	17.0%	21.9%	19.7%	17.4%	5.1%
From 2 to 5 years ago	5.6%	7.5%	8.7%	10.9%	7.1%	9.9%	7.3%
(Volunteered: Within 2 years)	0.2%	0.7%	0.4%	--	0.3%	1.1%	0.4%
(One or more on Q5)	71.8%	66.3%	65.0%	55.4%	54.8%	61.0%	83.5%
Total	100.0%	100.0%	100.0%	100.0%	100.0%	100.0%	100.0%
Valid weighted N	358	372	413	455	380	422	280

Chi-square test: p<.001

[Note to the reader: Q6b is a timeline check for respondents who said they had visited in their lifetime. Twenty respondents who initially reported that they had not visited within the past two years, but who volunteered on this question that they had, were put back into the pool of potential recent visitors, subject to later confirmation.]

---

[4] Number of units in the National Park System at the time of the survey.

Q6c. [If visited in past two years on item Q5 or Q6b, i.e., asked of respondents in the pool of potential visitors] **Which National Park System unit did you LAST visit?**

(Do NOT read unit names. As needed: It will take me a moment to look that up on my list. Do you know what state that's in? Is it in [state]? Is there any other name for it? Is it also called [name]? Can you spell it for me?)

Table Q6c.1. Frequency Distribution (national data, general public)

Response	Unweighted Frequency	Unweighted Percent	Weighted Percent
"Visitor" (Visited in past 2 years and named a unit found on list)	2,175	53.0%	46.5%
"Non-visitor" (All other respondents)	1,928	47.0%	53.5%
Total	4,103	100.0%	100.0%
Total N	4,103	4,103	2,706

Table Q6c.2. Cross-tabulation by Region (weighted regional data, general public)

Response	AKR	PWR	IMR	MWR	SER	NER	NCR
Visitor	60.0%	54.5%	49.7%	40.6%	39.1%	46.2%	70.6%
Non-visitor	40.0%	45.5%	50.3%	59.4%	60.9%	53.8%	29.4%
Total	100.0%	100.0%	100.0%	100.0%	100.0%	100.0%	100.0%
Total weighted N	362	376	422	465	389	426	283

Chi-square test: p<.001

[Note to the reader: Q6c provides the definition of visitor status used in the remainder of this report to compare visitors and non-visitors.

The interviewer confirmed whether the site visited most recently (within the past two years) was a valid NPS unit, by checking the site named by the respondent against a list previously verified by the NPS. The list was organized alphabetically by unit name, was cross-referenced by state, and included some common unit-name aliases. The interviewer probed for state, alternate name, and/or spelling, as needed, but no further probes or prompts were used at this point in the questionnaire.

For the rest of the interview, any respondent claiming to have visited in the past two years was asked the questions intended for visitors, even if the site visited was not found on the NPS list. However, final classification as a visitor was determined after data collection was completed, based on item Q6c. For purposes of this report, responses from persons who were ultimately classified as non-visitors are not shown in the tables on questions intended only for visitors.]

Q6d. [For all Non-visitors (as defined on item Q6c)] **A lot of people don't realize that the National Park System includes not only the big units like Yellowstone, but also national battlefields, national seashores, national recreation areas, and small urban sites. In your area [Unit Name 1] and [Unit Name 2] are both National Park System units. With this in mind, can you give me the name of any place you've visited in the past two years that you think is part of the National Park System?**

(As needed: My list might be missing some of the smaller units, so I'd like you to tell me any place you've visited in the past two years that you think is probably part of the National Park System. I can't find that on my list, so I'll just type it in. Can you repeat that for me? Can you spell it for me?)

Table Q6d.1. Frequency Distribution (national data, general public)

Response	Unweighted Frequency	Unweighted Percent	Weighted Percent
(Identified valid NPS unit on either on Q6c or Q6d)	2,780	67.8%	60.7%
(Identified no valid NPS unit visited within the past 2 years)	1,323	32.2%	39.3%
Total	4,103	100.0%	100.0%
Total N	4,103	4,103	2,706

Table Q6d.2. Cross-tabulation by Region (weighted regional data, general public)

Response	AKR	PWR	IMR	MWR	SER	NER	NCR
(Identified NPS unit)	73.7%	67.6%	62.0%	56.5%	55.5%	60.7%	85.0%
(No NPS unit)	26.3%	32.4%	38.0%	43.5%	44.5%	39.3%	15.0%
Total	100.0%	100.0%	100.0%	100.0%	100.0%	100.0%	100.0%
Total weighted N	362	376	422	465	389	426	284

Chi-square test: $p < .001$

[Note to the reader: Q6d could provide an alternative approach to measuring visitation, but this is NOT the definition of visitor status used in the remainder of the report.

The question included as a prompt the names of two NPS units in or near the respondent's state of residence, and also instructed the interviewer to take down verbatim the name or description of any site identified by the respondent that the interviewer could not find on the list. After data collection was completed, the open-ended responses on this item were coded as identifying valid or invalid NPS unit names, with results reflected in Tables Q6d.1 and Q6d.2, above.]

Q6e. [For all Visitors (as defined on item Q6c)] **So, we're calling** [Unit Name] **your most recent visit to a National Park System unit. Do I have that right?**

(If Yes, continue. If No, make a correction.)

Table Q6e.1. Frequency Distribution (recoded national data, recent visitors)

Response	Unweighted Frequency	Unweighted Percent	Weighted Percent
Denali NP	185	8.5%	1.4%
Grand Canyon NP	104	4.8%	6.5%
Great Smoky Mountains NP	60	2.8%	3.7%
Lincoln Memorial	79	3.6%	4.0%
National Mall	106	4.9%	2.1%
Yellowstone NP	126	5.8%	6.3%
Yosemite NP	109	5.0%	6.7%
Other NPS unit	1,406	64.6%	69.5%
Total valid	2,175	100.0%	100.0%
Non-visitor	1,928		
Total N	4,103	2,175	1,260

Table Q6e.2. Cross-tabulation by Region (weighted regional data, recent visitors)

Response	AKR	PWR	IMR	MWR	SER	NER	NCR
Denali NP	53.5%	2.1%	0.6%	1.1%	0.5%	1.1%	--
Grand Canyon NP	2.1%	5.4%	12.3%	7.9%	5.5%	1.8%	0.9%
Great Smoky Mtns	0.1%	--	1.0%	3.1%	13.3%	1.2%	--
Lincoln Memorial	1.3%	0.1%	1.6%	3.8%	1.3%	9.0%	8.8%
National Mall	--	0.2%	0.9%	1.1%	3.4%	4.2%	22.5%
Yellowstone NP	2.5%	5.1%	9.2%	7.8%	5.7%	3.9%	0.6%
Yosemite NP	1.1%	26.6%	1.7%	1.5%	2.4%	1.3%	0.3%
Other NPS unit	39.4%	60.5%	72.8%	73.6%	67.9%	77.6%	66.9%
Total	100.0%	100.0%	100.0%	100.0%	100.0%	100.0%	100.0%
Valid weighted N	216	204	209	189	153	198	201

Chi-square test: p<.001

25

Q7. Please tell us whether you strongly agree, somewhat agree, neither agree nor disagree, somewhat disagree, or strongly disagree with the following statement:

"I plan to visit a unit of the National Park System within the next 12 months."

Table Q7.1. Frequency Distribution (national data, general public)

Response	Unweighted Frequency	Unweighted Percent	Weighted Percent
Strongly agree	1,892	48.1%	43.3%
Somewhat agree	810	20.6%	23.5%
Neither agree nor disagree	185	4.7%	4.8%
Somewhat disagree	450	11.4%	13.5%
Strongly disagree	596	15.2%	14.9%
Total valid	3,933	100.0%	100.0%
(Don't know/Not sure)	155		
(No answer/Refused)	15		
Total missing	170		
Total N	4,103	3,933	2,601

Table Q7.2. Cross-tabulation by Visitation (weighted national data, recent visitors/non-visitors)

Response	Visitor	Non-visitor
Strongly agree	61.4%	27.4%
Somewhat agree	22.9%	24.0%
Neither	3.4%	6.1%
Somewhat disagree	6.3%	19.9%
Strongly disagree	6.0%	22.7%
Total	100.0%	100.0%
Valid weighted N	1,218	1,382

Chi-square test: p<.001

Table Q7.3. Cross-tabulation by Region (weighted regional data, general public)

Response	AKR	PWR	IMR	MWR	SER	NER	NCR
Strongly agree	55.7%	48.9%	46.8%	33.6%	40.3%	49.6%	66.5%
Somewhat agree	18.2%	22.5%	20.0%	25.5%	22.8%	21.0%	20.4%
Neither	3.8%	4.0%	5.8%	4.9%	4.5%	4.4%	2.7%
Somewhat disagree	9.7%	10.5%	12.7%	16.7%	13.6%	13.9%	3.4%
Strongly disagree	12.6%	14.1%	14.6%	19.3%	18.8%	11.2%	7.0%
Total	100.0%	100.0%	100.0%	100.0%	100.0%	100.0%	100.0%
Valid weighted N	347	362	404	450	377	403	280

Chi-square test: p<.001

Q8. [For random subset A] **We're interested in what kinds of vacation trips you like to take when you spend at least one night away from home. In the past two years, have you taken any overnight vacation trips away from home?**

Table Q8.1. Frequency Distribution (national data, general public)

Response	Unweighted Frequency	Unweighted Percent	Weighted Percent
Yes (recent vacation trip)	1,740	82.3%	81.2%
No	373	17.7%	18.8%
Total valid	2,113	100.0%	100.0%
(Don't know/Not sure)	3		
(No answer/Refused)	2		
(Not asked, random split)	1,985		
Total missing	1,990		
Total N	4,103	2,113	1,404

Table Q8.2. Cross-tabulation by Visitation (weighted national data, recent visitors/non-visitors)

Response	Visitor	Non-visitor
Yes (recent vacation trip)	92.9%	71.9%
No	7.1%	28.1%
Total	100.0%	100.0%
Valid weighted N	622	781

Chi-square test: p<.001

Q9. [For those in random subset A answering Yes on item Q8] **I'm going to list some different kinds of vacation trips that people might take. For each trip, please tell me how much you like it. Use a scale from one to four, where 1 means you "don't like it at all," 2 means you "like it very little," 3 means you "like it pretty much," and 4 means you "like it a lot." The first one is ...**

Q9a. [In random order] **An out-of-town trip to visit friends or relatives.**

(As needed: Would you say you "don't like this at all," "like it very little," "like it pretty much," or "like it a lot"?)

Table Q9a.1. Frequency Distribution (national data, general public who have taken a recent trip)

Response	Unweighted Frequency	Unweighted Percent	Weighted Percent
Don't like it at all	64	3.7%	2.9%
Like it very little	136	7.9%	7.5%
Like it pretty much	508	29.4%	31.1%
Like it a lot	1,021	59.1%	58.5%
Total valid	1,729	100.0%	100.0%
(Don't know/Not sure)	9		
(No answer/Refused)	2		
(No trips or missing on Q8)	378		
(Not asked, random split)	1,985		
Total missing	2,374		
Total N	4,103	1,729	1,135

Table Q9a.2. Cross-tabulation by Visitation (weighted national data, recent visitors/non-visitors who have taken a recent trip)

Response	Visitor	Non-visitor
Don't like it at all	2.4%	3.4%
Like it very little	7.6%	7.5%
Like it pretty much	33.0%	29.1%
Like it a lot	57.0%	60.0%
Total	100.0%	100.0%
Valid weighted N	577	558

Chi-square test: p>.2

Q9b. [In random order] **A trip to an out-of-town sporting event.**

Table Q9b.1. Frequency Distribution (national data, general public who have taken a recent trip)

Response	Unweighted Frequency	Unweighted Percent	Weighted Percent
Don't like it at all	519	30.3%	25.6%
Like it very little	413	24.1%	23.5%
Like it pretty much	414	24.2%	25.4%
Like it a lot	365	21.3%	25.5%
Total valid	1,711	100.0%	100.0%
(Don't know/Not sure)	23		
(No answer/Refused)	6		
(No trips or missing on Q8)	378		
(Not asked, random split)	1,985		
Total missing	2,392		
Total N	4,103	1,711	1,125

Table Q9b.2. Cross-tabulation by Visitation (weighted national data, recent visitors/non-visitors who have taken a recent trip)

Response	Visitor	Non-visitor
Don't like it at all	24.1%	27.1%
Like it very little	27.2%	19.7%
Like it pretty much	26.4%	24.3%
Like it a lot	22.2%	28.9%
Total	100.0%	100.0%
Valid weighted N	571	554

Chi-square test: $p < .01$

[Note to the reader: Q9c was eliminated during pretesting.]

Q9d. [In random order] **A trip to a theme park, such as Disney or Six Flags.**

Table Q9d.1. Frequency Distribution (national data, general public who have taken a recent trip)

Response	Unweighted Frequency	Unweighted Percent	Weighted Percent
Don't like it at all	443	25.7%	18.9%
Like it very little	404	23.5%	22.3%
Like it pretty much	411	23.9%	26.4%
Like it a lot	463	26.9%	32.5%
Total valid	1,721	100.0%	100.0%
(Don't know/Not sure)	18		
(No answer/Refused)	1		
(No trips or missing on Q8)	378		
(Not asked, random split)	1,985		
Total missing	2,382		
Total N	4,103	1,721	1,132

Table Q9d.2. Cross-tabulation by Visitation (weighted national data, recent visitors/non-visitors who have taken a recent trip)

Response	Visitor	Non-visitor
Don't like it at all	20.9%	16.8%
Like it very little	25.5%	19.0%
Like it pretty much	24.5%	28.3%
Like it a lot	29.1%	35.9%
Total	100.0%	100.0%
Valid weighted N	576	556

Chi-square test: p<.01

Q9e. [In random order] **A trip to experience art, music, or other cultural activities.**

Table Q9e.1. Frequency Distribution (national data, general public who have taken a recent trip)

Response	Unweighted Frequency	Unweighted Percent	Weighted Percent
Don't like it at all	149	8.6%	7.5%
Like it very little	318	18.5%	18.8%
Like it pretty much	591	34.3%	34.0%
Like it a lot	665	38.6%	39.7%
Total valid	1,723	100.0%	100.0%
(Don't know/Not sure)	13		
(No answer/Refused)	4		
(No trips or missing on Q8)	378		
(Not asked, random split)	1,985		
Total missing	2,380		
Total N	4,103	1,723	1,134

Table Q9e.2. Cross-tabulation by Visitation (weighted national data, recent visitors/non-visitors who have taken a recent trip)

Response	Visitor	Non-visitor
Don't like it at all	6.0%	9.0%
Like it very little	19.5%	18.1%
Like it pretty much	35.2%	32.8%
Like it a lot	39.4%	40.1%
Total	100.0%	100.0%
Valid weighted N	577	557

Chi-square test: p>.2

31

Q9f. [In random order] **An out-of-town trip to experience nature.**

Table Q9f.1. Frequency distribution (national data, general public who have taken a recent trip)

Response	Unweighted Frequency	Unweighted Percent	Weighted Percent
Don't like it at all	94	5.4%	4.6%
Like it very little	170	9.8%	11.5%
Like it pretty much	508	29.4%	30.7%
Like it a lot	957	55.3%	53.2%
Total valid	1,729	100.0%	100.0%
(Don't know/Not sure)	9		
(No answer/Refused)	2		
(No trips or missing on Q8)	378		
(Not asked, random split)	1,985		
Total missing	2,374		
Total N	4,103	1,729	1,136

Table Q9f.2. Cross-tabulation by visitation (weighted national data, recent visitors/non-visitors who have taken a recent trip)

Response	Visitor	Non-visitor
Don't like it at all	3.3%	5.9%
Like it very little	7.5%	15.7%
Like it pretty much	24.7%	36.8%
Like it a lot	64.6%	41.5%
Total	100.0%	100.0%
Valid weighted N	576	559

Chi-square test: p<.001

32

Q9g. [In random order] **A trip to see historical places or exhibits.**

Table Q9g.1. Frequency Distribution (national data, general public who have taken a recent trip)

Response	Unweighted Frequency	Unweighted Percent	Weighted Percent
Don't like it at all	61	3.5%	3.3%
Like it very little	202	11.7%	13.0%
Like it pretty much	667	38.7%	38.9%
Like it a lot	795	46.1%	44.8%
Total valid	1,725	100.0%	100.0%
(Don't know/Not sure)	13		
(No answer/Refused)	2		
(No trips or missing on Q8)	378		
(Not asked, random split)	1,985		
Total missing	2,378		
Total N	4,103	1,725	1,135

Table Q9g.2. Cross-tabulation by Visitation (weighted national data, recent visitors/non-visitors who have taken a recent trip)

Response	Visitor	Non-visitor
Don't like it at all	2.2%	4.5%
Like it very little	10.1%	16.0%
Like it pretty much	36.6%	41.2%
Like it a lot	51.1%	38.3%
Total	100.0%	100.0%
Valid weighted N	577	558

Chi-square test: p<.001

[Note to the reader: Q9h was eliminated during pretesting.]

Q9i. [In random order] **A trip to a casino or other gaming place.**

Table Q9i.1. Frequency Distribution (national data, general public who have taken a recent trip)

Response	Unweighted Frequency	Unweighted Percent	Weighted Percent
Don't like it at all	884	51.3%	48.0%
Like it very little	355	20.6%	22.0%
Like it pretty much	248	14.4%	15.2%
Like it a lot	237	13.7%	14.9%
Total valid	1,724	100.0%	100.0%
(Don't know/Not sure)	13		
(No answer/Refused)	3		
(No trips or missing on Q8)	378		
(Not asked, random split)	1,985		
Total missing	2,379		
Total N	4,103	1,724	1,130

Table Q9i.2. Cross-tabulation by Visitation (weighted national data, recent visitors/non-visitors who have taken a recent trip)

Response	Visitor	Non-visitor
Don't like it at all	53.0%	42.9%
Like it very little	21.0%	22.9%
Like it pretty much	14.4%	15.9%
Like it a lot	11.6%	18.3%
Total	100.0%	100.0%
Valid weighted N	573	558

Chi-square test: p<.01

34

Q9j. [In random order] **A trip to another country.**

Table Q9j.1. Frequency Distribution (national data, general public who have taken a recent trip)

Response	Unweighted Frequency	Unweighted Percent	Weighted Percent
Don't like it at all	250	14.7%	14.0%
Like it very little	157	9.2%	9.8%
Like it pretty much	297	17.5%	17.4%
Like it a lot	995	58.6%	58.8%
Total valid	1,699	100.0%	100.0%
(Don't know/Not sure)	33		
(No answer/Refused)	8		
(No trips or missing on Q8)	378		
(Not asked, random split)	1,985		
Total missing	2,404		
Total N	4,103	1,699	1,119

Table Q9j.2. Cross-tabulation by Visitation (weighted national data, recent visitors/non-visitors who have taken a recent trip)

Response	Visitor	Non-visitor
Don't like it at all	13.6%	14.4%
Like it very little	9.5%	10.1%
Like it pretty much	18.6%	16.3%
Like it a lot	58.3%	59.2%
Total	100.0%	100.0%
Valid weighted N	570	550

Chi-square test: p>.2

Q9k. [In random order] **A trip to a spa or resort.**

Table Q9k.1. Frequency Distribution (national data, general public who have taken a recent trip)

Response	Unweighted Frequency	Unweighted Percent	Weighted Percent
Don't like it at all	388	23.0%	19.4%
Like it very little	387	22.9%	19.8%
Like it pretty much	422	25.0%	27.4%
Like it a lot	493	29.2%	33.4%
Total valid	1,690	100.0%	100.0%
(Don't know/Not sure)	45		
(No answer/Refused)	5		
(No trips or missing on Q8)	378		
(Not asked, random split)	1,985		
Total missing	2,413		
Total N	4,103	1,690	1,111

Table Q9k.2. Cross-tabulation by Visitation (weighted national data, recent visitors/non-visitors who have taken a recent trip)

Response	Visitor	Non-visitor
Don't like it at all	19.9%	18.8%
Like it very little	23.7%	15.8%
Like it pretty much	29.3%	25.4%
Like it a lot	27.1%	39.9%
Total	100.0%	100.0%
Valid weighted N	561	549

Chi-square test: p<.001

Q9l. [In random order] **A trip on a cruise ship.**

Table Q9l.1. Frequency Distribution (national data, general public who have taken a recent trip)

Response	Unweighted Frequency	Unweighted Percent	Weighted Percent
Don't like it at all	519	31.5%	25.8%
Like it very little	351	21.3%	20.3%
Like it pretty much	304	18.4%	21.0%
Like it a lot	475	28.8%	32.9%
Total valid	1,649	100.0%	100.0%
(Don't know/Not sure)	80		
(No answer/Refused)	11		
(No trips or missing on Q8)	378		
(Not asked, random split)	1,985		
Total missing	2,454		
Total N	4,103	1,649	1,092

Table Q9l.2. Cross-tabulation by Visitation (weighted national data, recent visitors/non-visitors who have taken a recent trip)

Response	Visitor	Non-visitor
Don't like it at all	30.3%	21.4%
Like it very little	20.8%	19.7%
Like it pretty much	19.4%	22.6%
Like it a lot	29.5%	36.3%
Total	100.0%	100.0%
Valid weighted N	546	546

Chi-square test: p<.01

Q10. [For all Visitors] **Now I'd like to ask you a series of questions about your last visit to a National Park System unit, which you said was** [Unit Name]. **Thinking about your last visit to** [Unit Name]**, what were your two or three main reasons for visiting there?**

(Do NOT read choices; code up to 3 responses.)

Table Q10.1. Multiple Response Frequencies (national data, recent visitors)

Response	Unweighted Frequency	Unweighted Percent	Weighted Percent
Sightseeing	922	42.5%	42.8%
Vacationing with guests, family, company, relatives	652	30.1%	33.8%
Viewing exhibits, park information, educational sites	231	10.7%	11.8%
Hiking or backpacking	240	11.1%	10.7%
Go just because it's there, proximity	510	23.5%	23.0%
Camping	89	4.1%	5.0%
Visiting a cultural or historic site	298	13.7%	16.2%
Playing sports, recreation, exercise, dog walking	127	5.9%	5.8%
Fishing	49	2.3%	1.8%
Viewing or photographing nature/wildlife/ birds/trees/flowers	369	17.0%	13.6%
Other	713	32.9%	31.6%
(Don't know/Not sure)	7		
Total N	2,175	2,168	1,258

This is a mark-up-to-three question; percentages total more than 100.

Table Q10.2. Multiple Response Frequencies by Region (weighted regional data, recent visitors)

Response	AKR	PWR	IMR	MWR	SER	NER	NCR
Sightseeing	55.2%	47.7%	47.2%	43.3%	44.3%	33.2%	28.4%
Vacationing with guests, family, company, relatives	28.6%	39.2%	32.4%	36.6%	29.0%	32.6%	25.5%
Viewing exhibits, park information, educational sites	6.3%	10.2%	11.3%	10.5%	11.9%	14.9%	10.5%
Hiking or backpacking	8.5%	17.5%	11.6%	5.1%	12.2%	9.1%	10.3%
Go just because it's there, proximity	22.7%	19.7%	25.9%	22.3%	25.4%	23.9%	28.0%
Camping	4.9%	9.2%	4.9%	5.6%	3.4%	2.8%	1.5%
Visiting a cultural or historic site	3.0%	7.1%	11.0%	19.9%	12.6%	24.0%	18.4%
Playing sports, recreation, exercise, dog walking	4.4%	5.1%	3.2%	7.8%	4.6%	6.0%	9.8%
Fishing	3.7%	1.9%	2.1%	1.4%	2.4%	0.8%	0.5%
Viewing or photographing nature/wildlife/birds/trees/flowers	32.0%	21.6%	13.9%	11.5%	14.0%	11.3%	13.6%
Other	26.1%	28.7%	29.0%	33.1%	32.3%	33.3%	43.5%
Valid weighted N	215	205	210	189	151	197	200

This is a mark-up-to-three question; percentages total more than 100 within each region.

Q11. [For Visitors in random subset B] **We'd like to know how much the following experiences may have added to your enjoyment during your last visit to [Unit Name]. Please rate each one on a scale from one to four, where 1 means it "added nothing to your enjoyment," 2 means it "added very little to your enjoyment," 3 means it "added pretty much to your enjoyment," and 4 means it "added a lot to your enjoyment" on your last visit there.**

Q11a. [In random order] **Learning more about history and culture.**

(As needed: Would you say it added "nothing," "very little," "pretty much," or "a lot" to your enjoyment, on your last visit to a unit of the National Park System?)

Table Q11a. Frequency Distribution (national data, recent visitors)

Response	Unweighted Frequency	Unweighted Percent	Weighted Percent
Nothing	115	10.7%	8.2%
Very little	179	16.7%	15.7%
Pretty much	297	27.7%	29.5%
A lot	483	45.0%	46.7%
Total valid	1,074	100.0%	100.0%
(Don't know/Not sure)	6		
(No answer/Refused)	2		
(Not asked, random split)	1,093		
Total missing	1,101		
Total N	2,175	1,074	634

Q11b. [In random order] **Learning more about nature.**

Table Q11b. Frequency Distribution (national data, recent visitors)

Response	Unweighted Frequency	Unweighted Percent	Weighted Percent
Nothing	145	13.6%	12.0%
Very little	202	19.0%	18.7%
Pretty much	339	31.8%	32.1%
A lot	379	35.6%	37.3%
Total valid	1,065	100.0%	100.0%
(Don't know/Not sure)	14		
(No answer/Refused)	3		
(Not asked, random split)	1,093		
Total missing	1,110		
Total N	2,175	1,065	628

Q11c. [In random order] **Getting exercise.**

Table Q11c. Frequency Distribution (national data, recent visitors)

Response	Unweighted Frequency	Unweighted Percent	Weighted Percent
Nothing	96	9.0%	8.1%
Very little	179	16.7%	15.0%
Pretty much	293	27.4%	29.0%
A lot	501	46.9%	47.9%
Total valid	1,069	100.0%	100.0%
(Don't know/Not sure)	8		
(No answer/Refused)	5		
(Not asked, random split)	1,093		
Total missing	1,106		
Total N	2,175	1,069	631

Q11d. [In random order] **Getting away from the noise back home.**

Table Q11d. Frequency Distribution (national data, recent visitors)

Response	Unweighted Frequency	Unweighted Percent	Weighted Percent
Nothing	150	14.2%	11.2%
Very little	134	12.7%	10.8%
Pretty much	227	21.5%	21.4%
A lot	544	51.6%	56.6%
Total valid	1,055	100.0%	100.0%
(Don't know/Not sure)	21		
(No answer/Refused)	6		
(Not asked, random split)	1,093		
Total missing	1,120		
Total N	2,175	1,055	630

Q11e. [In random order] **Getting away from the bright lights back home.**

Table Q11e. Frequency Distribution (national data, recent visitors)

Response	Unweighted Frequency	Unweighted Percent	Weighted Percent
Nothing	191	18.2%	15.3%
Very little	138	13.1%	12.1%
Pretty much	199	18.9%	20.4%
A lot	523	49.8%	52.2%
Total valid	1,051	100.0%	100.0%
(Don't know/Not sure)	28		
(No answer/Refused)	3		
(Not asked, random split)	1,093		
Total missing	1,124		
Total N	2,175	1,051	628

Q11f. [In random order] **Seeing distant or unobstructed views.**

Table Q11f. Frequency Distribution (national data, recent visitors)

Response	Unweighted Frequency	Unweighted Percent	Weighted Percent
Nothing	85	8.0%	6.6%
Very little	85	8.0%	7.6%
Pretty much	255	23.9%	27.4%
A lot	644	60.2%	58.4%
Total valid	1,069	100.0%	100.0%
(Don't know/Not sure)	10		
(No answer/Refused)	3		
(Not asked, random split)	1,093		
Total missing	1,106		
Total N	2,175	1,069	631

Q11g. [In random order] **Hearing the sounds of nature.**

Table Q11g. Frequency Distribution (national data, recent visitors)

Response	Unweighted Frequency	Unweighted Percent	Weighted Percent
Nothing	129	12.0%	11.7%
Very little	144	13.4%	12.3%
Pretty much	268	25.0%	25.7%
A lot	530	49.5%	50.3%
Total valid	1,071	100.0%	100.0%
(Don't know/Not sure)	10		
(No answer/Refused)	1		
(Not asked, random split)	1,093		
Total missing	1,104		
Total N	2,175	1,071	629

Q11h. [In random order] **Relaxing physically.**

Table Q11h. Frequency Distribution (national data, recent visitors)

Response	Unweighted Frequency	Unweighted Percent	Weighted Percent
Nothing	67	6.2%	5.6%
Very little	127	11.8%	9.0%
Pretty much	320	29.8%	29.8%
A lot	559	52.1%	55.6%
Total valid	1,073	100.0%	100.0%
(Don't know/Not sure)	8		
(No answer/Refused)	1		
(Not asked, random split)	1,093		
Total missing	1,102		
Total N	2,175	1,073	631

Q11i. [In random order] **Viewing the sights of nature.**

Table Q11i. Frequency Distribution (national data, recent visitors)

Response	Unweighted Frequency	Unweighted Percent	Weighted Percent
Nothing	82	7.6%	6.3%
Very little	78	7.3%	6.7%
Pretty much	191	17.8%	18.9%
A lot	722	67.3%	68.1%
Total valid	1,073	100.0%	100.0%
(Don't know/Not sure)	8		
(No answer/Refused)	1		
(Not asked, random split)	1,093		
Total missing	1,102		
Total N	2,175	1,073	630

[Note to the reader: Questions 12 and 13 were eliminated during pretesting.]

Q14. [For all Visitors] **On your last visit to** [Unit Name] **did you or any member of your personal group participate in any of the following in the park?**

(As needed: Your personal group includes any friends or relatives you may have been traveling with when you visited. If you were part of a large tour group, your personal group does not include people you did not know before the tour.)

[Note to the reader: Q14a was eliminated during pretesting.]

Q14b. [In random order] **Hiking or jogging for at least 30 continuous minutes.**

(As needed: On your last visit, did any member of your personal group do this?)

Table Q14b.1. Frequency Distribution (national data, recent visitors)

Response	Unweighted Frequency	Unweighted Percent	Weighted Percent
Yes (did this)	1,266	58.3%	59.9%
No	904	41.7%	40.1%
Total valid	2,170	100.0%	100.0%
(Don't know/Not sure)	5		
(No answer/Refused)	0		
Total missing	5		
Total N	2,175	2,170	1,258

Table Q14b.2. Cross-tabulation by Region (weighted regional data, recent visitors)

Response	AKR	PWR	IMR	MWR	SER	NER	NCR
Yes (did this)	61.8%	72.9%	65.2%	54.3%	62.3%	48.8%	41.4%
No	38.2%	27.1%	34.8%	45.7%	37.7%	51.2%	58.6%
Total	100.0%	100.0%	100.0%	100.0%	100.0%	100.0%	100.0%
Valid wtd. N	215	205	210	189	151	197	200

Chi-square test: p<.001

Q14c. [In random order] **Viewing or photographing animals or plants.**

Table Q14c.1. Frequency Distribution (national data, recent visitors)

Response	Unweighted Frequency	Unweighted Percent	Weighted Percent
Yes (did this)	1,463	67.5%	69.6%
No	704	32.5%	30.4%
Total valid	2,167	100.0%	100.0%
(Don't know/Not sure)	8		
(No answer/Refused)	0		
Total missing	8		
Total N	2,175	2,167	1,256

Table Q14c.2. Cross-tabulation by Region (weighted regional data, recent visitors)

Response	AKR	PWR	IMR	MWR	SER	NER	NCR
Yes (did this)	83.3%	85.0%	76.2%	66.1%	71.5%	55.8%	40.9%
No	16.7%	15.0%	23.8%	33.9%	28.5%	44.2%	59.1%
Total	100.0%	100.0%	100.0%	100.0%	100.0%	100.0%	100.0%
Valid wtd. N	217	205	209	189	151	197	199

Chi-square test: p<.001

[Note to the reader: Q14d was eliminated during pretesting.]

Q14e. [In random order] **Snow sports, such as skiing, snowmobiling, or sledding.**

Table Q14e.1. Frequency Distribution (national data, recent visitors)

Response	Unweighted Frequency	Unweighted Percent	Weighted Percent
Yes (did this)	120	5.5%	4.9%
No	2,054	94.5%	95.1%
Total valid	2,174	100.0%	100.0%
(Don't know/Not sure)	1		
(No answer/Refused)	0		
Total missing	1		
Total N	2,175	2,174	1,259

Table Q14e.2. Cross-tabulation by Region (weighted regional data, recent visitors)

Response	AKR	PWR	IMR	MWR	SER	NER	NCR
Yes (did this)	12.5%	9.1%	8.7%	1.8%	2.5%	2.0%	2.1%
No	87.5%	90.9%	91.3%	98.2%	97.5%	98.0%	97.9%
Total	100.0%	100.0%	100.0%	100.0%	100.0%	100.0%	100.0%
Valid wtd. N	217	205	209	189	153	197	200

Chi-square test: p<.001

Q14f. [In random order] **Water activities, such as swimming or boating.**

Table Q14f.1. Frequency Distribution (national data, recent visitors)

Response	Unweighted Frequency	Unweighted Percent	Weighted Percent
Yes (did this)	391	18.0%	20.2%
No	1,781	82.0%	79.8%
Total valid	2,172	100.0%	100.0%
(Don't know/Not sure)	2		
(No answer/Refused)	1		
Total missing	3		
Total N	2,175	2,172	1,257

Table Q14f.2. Cross-tabulation by Region (weighted regional data, recent visitors)

Response	AKR	PWR	IMR	MWR	SER	NER	NCR
Yes (did this)	23.1%	22.4%	19.6%	18.7%	26.7%	17.8%	8.4%
No	76.9%	77.6%	80.4%	81.3%	73.3%	82.2%	91.6%
Total	100.0%	100.0%	100.0%	100.0%	100.0%	100.0%	100.0%
Valid wtd. N	217	205	208	189	153	197	201

Chi-square test: p<.001

Q15. [For all Visitors] **On your last visit to** [Unit Name] **did you or any member of your personal group use any of the following programs or services?**

(As needed: Your personal group includes any friends or relatives you may have been traveling with when you visited. If you were part of a large tour group, your personal group does not include people you did not know before the tour.)

Q15a. [In random order] **Attend a ranger-led activity, such as a tour or talk.**

(As needed: On your last visit, did any member of your person group do this?)

Table Q15a.1. Frequency Distribution (national data, recent visitors)

Response	Unweighted Frequency	Unweighted Percent	Weighted Percent
Yes (did this)	720	33.4%	34.9%
No	1,438	66.6%	65.1%
Total valid	2,158	100.0%	100.0%
(Don't know/Not sure)	14		
(No answer/Refused)	3		
Total missing	17		
Total N	2,175	2,158	1,248

Table Q15a.2. Cross-tabulation by Region (weighted regional data, recent visitors)

Response	AKR	PWR	IMR	MWR	SER	NER	NCR
Yes	36.3%	30.9%	32.7%	38.6%	39.0%	33.1%	22.4%
No	63.7%	69.1%	67.3%	61.4%	61.0%	66.9%	77.6%
Total	100.0%	100.0%	100.0%	100.0%	100.0%	100.0%	100.0%
Valid wtd. N	215	204	208	189	149	195	200

Chi-square test: p<.05

Q15b. [In random order] **Talk informally with a ranger.**

Table Q15b.1. Frequency Distribution (national data, recent visitors)

Response	Unweighted Frequency	Unweighted Percent	Weighted Percent
Yes (did this)	1,076	49.9%	50.8%
No	1,079	50.1%	49.2%
Total valid	2,155	100.0%	100.0%
(Don't know/Not sure)	19		
(No answer/Refused)	1		
Total missing	20		
Total N	2,175	2,155	1,249

Table Q15b.2. Cross-tabulation by Region (weighted regional data, recent visitors)

Response	AKR	PWR	IMR	MWR	SER	NER	NCR
Yes (did this)	60.8%	52.9%	51.2%	53.1%	53.8%	43.7%	23.8%
No	39.2%	47.1%	48.8%	46.9%	46.2%	56.3%	76.2%
Total	100.0%	100.0%	100.0%	100.0%	100.0%	100.0%	100.0%
Valid wtd. N	214	205	205	188	151	196	199

Chi-square test: p<.001

Q15c. [In random order] **View outdoor exhibits.**

Table Q15c.1. Frequency Distribution (national data, recent visitors)

Response	Unweighted Frequency	Unweighted Percent	Weighted Percent
Yes (did this)	1,624	75.2%	78.4%
No	537	24.8%	21.6%
Total valid	2,161	100.0%	100.0%
(Don't know/Not sure)	13		
(No answer/Refused)	1		
Total missing	14		
Total N	2,175	2,161	1,255

Table Q15c.2. Cross-tabulation by Region (weighted regional data, recent visitors)

Response	AKR	PWR	IMR	MWR	SER	NER	NCR
Yes (did this)	72.8%	74.8%	77.4%	83.6%	84.2%	74.0%	62.7%
No	27.2%	25.2%	22.6%	16.4%	15.8%	26.0%	37.3%
Total	100.0%	100.0%	100.0%	100.0%	100.0%	100.0%	100.0%
Valid wtd. N	214	204	208	189	152	196	199

Chi-square test: p<.001

Q15d. [In random order] **View indoor exhibits.**

Table Q15d.1. Frequency Distribution (national data, recent visitors)

Response	Unweighted Frequency	Unweighted Percent	Weighted Percent
Yes (did this)	1,300	60.0%	62.7%
No	866	40.0%	37.3%
Total valid	2,166	100.0%	100.0%
(Don't know/Not sure)	8		
(No answer/Refused)	1		
Total missing	9		
Total N	2,175	2,166	1,255

Table Q15d.2. Cross-tabulation by Region (weighted regional data, recent visitors)

Response	AKR	PWR	IMR	MWR	SER	NER	NCR
Yes (did this)	60.0%	64.6%	63.9%	62.6%	59.0%	64.7%	40.3%
No	40.0%	35.4%	36.1%	37.4%	41.0%	35.3%	59.7%
Total	100.0%	100.0%	100.0%	100.0%	100.0%	100.0%	100.0%
Valid wtd. N	214	204	208	189	152	196	200

Chi-square test: p<.001

Q15e. [In random order] **Attend a cultural demonstration or performance.**

Table Q15e.1. Frequency Distribution (national data, recent visitors)

Response	Unweighted Frequency	Unweighted Percent	Weighted Percent
Yes (did this)	478	22.0%	20.9%
No	1,691	78.0%	79.1%
Total valid.	2,169	100.0%	100.0%
(Don't know/Not sure)	6		
(No answer/Refused)	0		
Total missing	6		
Total N	2,175	2,169	1,254

Table Q15e.2. Cross-tabulation by Region (weighted regional data, recent visitors)

Response	AKR	PWR	IMR	MWR	SER	NER	NCR
Yes (did this)	19.4%	19.0%	22.8%	17.8%	21.5%	21.8%	29.5%
No	80.6%	81.0%	77.2%	82.2%	78.5%	78.2%	70.5%
Total	100.0%	100.0%	100.0%	100.0%	100.0%	100.0%	100.0%
Valid wtd. N	217	205	209	189	152	196	200

Chi-square test: p=.097

Q15f. [In random order] **Read the park brochure or newspaper.**

Table Q15f.1. Frequency Distribution (national data, recent visitors)

Response	Unweighted Frequency	Unweighted Percent	Weighted Percent
Yes (did this)	1,602	74.1%	78.0%
No	559	25.9%	22.0%
Total valid	2,161	100.0%	100.0%
(Don't know/Not sure)	13		
(No answer/Refused)	1		
Total missing	14		
Total N	2,175	2,161	1,252

Table Q15f.2. Cross-tabulation by Region (weighted regional data, recent visitors)

Response	AKR	PWR	IMR	MWR	SER	NER	NCR
Yes (did this)	71.9%	81.3%	82.6%	83.1%	76.2%	69.7%	54.2%
No	28.1%	18.7%	17.4%	16.9%	23.8%	30.3%	45.8%
Total	100.0%	100.0%	100.0%	100.0%	100.0%	100.0%	100.0%
Valid wtd. N	216	204	208	188	151	195	199

Chi-square test: p<.001

Q15g. [In random order] **Go to the visitor center.**

Table Q15g.1. Frequency Distribution (national data, recent visitors)

Response	Unweighted Frequency	Unweighted Percent	Weighted Percent
Yes (did this)	1,537	71.2%	72.8%
No	621	28.8%	27.2%
Total valid	2,158	100.0%	100.0%
(Don't know/Not sure)	16		
(No answer/Refused)	1		
Total missing	17		
Total N	2,175	2,158	1,250

Table Q15g.2. Cross-tabulation by Region (weighted regional data, recent visitors)

Response	AKR	PWR	IMR	MWR	SER	NER	NCR
Yes (did this)	78.3%	77.4%	78.6%	75.1%	69.5%	67.6%	45.5%
No	21.7%	22.6%	21.4%	24.9%	30.5%	32.4%	54.5%
Total	100.0%	100.0%	100.0%	100.0%	100.0%	100.0%	100.0%
Valid wtd. N	216	203	210	185	151	195	200

Chi-square test: p<.001

Q15h. [In random order] **Watch movies or videos about the park.**

Table Q15h.1. Frequency Distribution (national data, recent visitors)

Response	Unweighted Frequency	Unweighted Percent	Weighted Percent
Yes (did this)	793	36.8%	38.9%
No	1,363	63.2%	61.1%
Total valid	2,156	100.0%	100.0%
(Don't know/Not sure)	18		
(No answer/Refused)	1		
Total missing	19		
Total N	2,175	2,156	1,250

Table Q15h.2. Cross-tabulation by Region (weighted regional data, recent visitors)

Response	AKR	PWR	IMR	MWR	SER	NER	NCR
Yes (did this)	42.6%	32.7%	37.2%	41.3%	40.4%	40.4%	16.5%
No	57.4%	67.3%	62.8%	58.7%	59.6%	59.6%	83.5%
Total	100.0%	100.0%	100.0%	100.0%	100.0%	100.0%	100.0%
Valid wtd. N	215	205	206	186	152	195	200

Chi-square test: p<.001

Q15i. [In random order] **Have any involvement with the Junior Ranger program.**

Table Q15i.1. Frequency Distribution (national data, recent visitors)

Response	Unweighted Frequency	Unweighted Percent	Weighted Percent
Yes (did this)	79	3.6%	3.5%
No	2,087	96.4%	96.5%
Total valid	2,166	100.0%	100.0%
(Don't know/Not sure)	9		
(No answer/Refused)	0		
Total missing	9		
Total N	2,175	2,166	1,257

Table Q15i.2. Cross-tabulation by Region (weighted regional data, recent visitors)

Response	AKR	PWR	IMR	MWR	SER	NER	NCR
Yes (did this)	8.8%	5.6%	4.0%	2.7%	3.9%	1.5%	0.5%
No	91.2%	94.4%	96.0%	97.3%	96.1%	98.5%	99.5%
Total	100.0%	100.0%	100.0%	100.0%	100.0%	100.0%	100.0%
Valid wtd. N	215	204	209	189	152	197	200

Chi-square test: p<.001

Q15j. [For Visitors answering Yes on at least two of Q15a-i] **Which ONE of those programs or services added the most enjoyment to your visit to** [Unit Name]?

(Do NOT read choices; code ONE response.)

Table Q15j.1. Frequency Distribution (national data, recent visitors with multiple activities)

Response	Unweighted Frequency	Unweighted Percent	Weighted Percent
Attending a cultural demonstration or performance	67	3.8%	2.6%
Attending a ranger-led activity, such as a tour or talk	272	15.6%	17.0%
Going to the visitor center	234	13.4%	11.9%
Having any involvement with the Junior Ranger program	17	1.0%	1.0%
Reading the park brochure or newspaper	102	5.8%	5.7%
Talking informally with a ranger	242	13.8%	13.4%
Viewing INDOOR exhibits	125	7.1%	7.4%
Viewing OUTDOOR exhibits	379	21.7%	21.9%
Watching movies or videos about the park	79	4.5%	5.1%
Other	232	13.3%	14.0%
Total valid	1,749	100.0%	100.0%
(Don't know/Not sure)	93		
(No answer/Refused)	12		
(No activities on Q15a-i)	139		
(Only one activity on Q15a-i)	182		
Total missing	426		
Total N	2,175	1,749	1,041

Table Q15j.2. Cross-tabulation by Region (weighted regional data, recent visitors with multiple activities)

Response	AKR	PWR	IMR	MWR	SER	NER	NCR
Attending a cultural demonstration or performance	2.7%	1.5%	3.4%	1.4%	4.0%	3.0%	9.9%
Attending a ranger-led activity, such as a tour or talk	15.7%	17.3%	14.0%	19.3%	19.6%	14.0%	11.7%
Going to the visitor center	16.4%	16.6%	14.0%	9.4%	5.5%	12.5%	8.9%
Having any involvement with the Junior Ranger program	1.4%	1.4%	1.5%	0.7%	1.7%	--	0.2%
Reading the park brochure or newspaper	5.6%	5.1%	5.7%	7.1%	4.2%	4.8%	8.9%
Talking informally with a ranger	19.2%	11.3%	11.3%	11.2%	15.4%	16.0%	7.4%
Viewing INDOOR exhibits	3.0%	7.8%	7.2%	6.2%	7.5%	9.5%	10.7%
Viewing OUTDOOR exhibits	20.2%	21.7%	24.8%	23.0%	25.2%	19.0%	29.1%
Watching movies or videos about the park	3.1%	3.4%	4.6%	4.3%	3.7%	8.1%	2.2%
Other	12.6%	14.0%	13.5%	17.5%	13.2%	13.1%	11.0%
Total	100%	100%	100%	100%	100%	100%	100%
Valid weighted N	181	171	178	156	127	160	134

Chi-square test: p<.05

Q16. [For Visitors in random subset A] **We'd like to know how you traveled from your home to the park on your last visit to [Unit Name]. I'll read you a short list. Please tell me all forms of transportation you used to reach the park on that visit. Did you use ...**

(Read choices, one at a time; mark ALL that the respondent mentions.)

Table Q16. Multiple Response Frequencies (national data, recent visitors)

Response	Unweighted Frequency	Unweighted Percent	Weighted Percent
Car, truck, or SUV	866	79.4%	83.7%
Recreational vehicle or motor home	46	4.2%	5.1%
Airplane	163	15.0%	14.7%
Tour bus or tour van	69	6.3%	6.6%
City bus or subway	94	8.6%	6.9%
Train or long-distance passenger bus	36	3.3%	3.2%
Cruise ship or other water transportation	33	3.0%	3.2%
Any other means of transportation	57	5.2%	5.4%
(None of the above -- only walked to/only ran to/live within the park)	26	2.4%	0.2%
(Don't know/Not sure)	3		
(No answer/Refused)	0		
(Not asked, random split)	1,082		
Total missing	1,085		
Total N	2,175	1,090	622

This is a mark-all-that-apply question; percentages total more than 100.

Q16a. [For Visitors in random subset A answering Car/Truck/SUV or RV on Q16] **For that visit, did you use any kind of rented vehicles to reach the park?**

Table Q16a. Frequency Distribution (national data, recent visitors who used a vehicle)

Response	Unweighted Frequency	Unweighted Percent	Weighted Percent
Yes (rental vehicle)	129	14.6%	15.0%
No	756	85.4%	85.0%
Total valid	885	100.0%	100.0%
(Don't know/Not sure)	0		
(No answer/Refused)	0		
(Not asked, no car or RV on Q16)	208		
(Not asked, random split)	1,082		
Total missing	1,290		
Total N	2,175	885	534

Q17. **Now we're interested in why people don't visit National Park System units more often. I'm going to read a series of statements. I'd like you to think of your own experiences, and tell me if you strongly agree, somewhat agree, neither agree nor disagree, somewhat disagree, or strongly disagree with each statement:**

Q17a. [In random order] **"Entrance fees are too high at National Park System units."**

(As needed: Would you say you "strongly agree," "somewhat agree,""neither agree nor disagree," "somewhat disagree," or "strongly disagree"?)

Table Q17a.1. Frequency Distribution (national data, general public)

Response	Unweighted Frequency	Unweighted Percent	Weighted Percent
Strongly agree	314	8.7%	8.8%
Somewhat agree	526	14.5%	15.0%
Neither agree nor disagree	349	9.6%	10.5%
Somewhat disagree	1,060	29.3%	30.5%
Strongly disagree	1,369	37.8%	35.1%
Total valid	3,618	100.0%	100.0%
(Don't know/Not sure)	469		
(No answer/Refused)	16		
Total missing	485		
Total N	4,103	3,618	2,391

Table Q17a.2. Cross-tabulation by Visitation (weighted national data, recent visitors/non-visitors)

Response	Visitor	Non-visitor
Strongly agree	5.9%	11.8%
Somewhat agree	13.7%	16.4%
Neither	8.6%	12.5%
Somewhat disagree	30.4%	30.7%
Strongly disagree	41.3%	28.6%
Total	100.0%	100.0%
Valid weighted N	1,221	1,169

Chi-square test: p<.001

Table Q17a.3. Cross-tabulation by Region (weighted regional data, general public)

Response	AKR	PWR	IMR	MWR	SER	NER	NCR
Strongly agree	9.0%	15.1%	12.4%	8.3%	10.5%	5.3%	7.7%
Somewhat agree	14.6%	14.9%	18.7%	14.4%	11.5%	17.4%	10.1%
Neither	11.7%	10.2%	10.6%	11.4%	9.1%	10.8%	4.3%
Somewhat disagree	30.7%	26.2%	27.3%	33.0%	32.4%	27.9%	30.1%
Strongly disagree	34.1%	33.7%	31.1%	32.9%	36.4%	38.6%	47.8%
Total	100.0%	100.0%	100.0%	100.0%	100.0%	100.0%	100.0%
Valid weighted N	325	331	375	412	342	373	265

Chi-square test: p<.001

Q17b. [In random order] **"The hotel and food costs at National Park System units are too high."**

Table Q17b.1. Frequency Distribution (national data, general public)

Response	Unweighted Frequency	Unweighted Percent	Weighted Percent
Strongly agree	590	18.1%	18.5%
Somewhat agree	761	23.3%	22.6%
Neither agree nor disagree	538	16.5%	16.5%
Somewhat disagree	810	24.8%	25.5%
Strongly disagree	568	17.4%	16.8%
Total valid	3,267	100.0%	100.0%
(Don't know/Not sure)	800		
(No answer/Refused)	36		
Total missing	836		
Total N	4,103	3,267	2,208

Table Q17b.2. Cross-tabulation by Visitation (weighted national data, recent visitors/non-visitors)

Response	Visitor	Non-visitor
Strongly agree	12.6%	24.6%
Somewhat agree	23.7%	21.6%
Neither	15.7%	17.3%
Somewhat disagree	28.5%	22.5%
Strongly disagree	19.5%	14.1%
Total	100.0%	100.0%
Valid weighted N	1,111	1,099

Chi-square test: p<.001

Table Q17b.3. Cross-tabulation by Region (weighted regional data, general public)

Response	AKR	PWR	IMR	MWR	SER	NER	NCR
Strongly agree	23.1%	23.0%	23.8%	16.0%	21.2%	16.0%	15.9%
Somewhat agree	28.4%	24.1%	22.4%	24.3%	19.0%	24.4%	23.2%
Neither	19.4%	15.7%	14.8%	18.2%	14.2%	18.1%	13.6%
Somewhat disagree	17.1%	24.2%	23.1%	25.9%	27.1%	24.7%	25.5%
Strongly disagree	12.1%	13.0%	15.8%	15.6%	18.6%	16.7%	21.8%
Total	100.0%	100.0%	100.0%	100.0%	100.0%	100.0%	100.0%
Valid weighted N	293	303	344	374	317	341	235

Chi-square test: p<.01

Q17c. [In random order] "**National Park System units are not safe places to visit.**"

Table Q17c.1. Frequency Distribution (national data, general public)

Response	Unweighted Frequency	Unweighted Percent	Weighted Percent
Strongly agree	89	2.3%	2.5%
Somewhat agree	145	3.7%	4.0%
Neither agree nor disagree	132	3.4%	3.2%
Somewhat disagree	828	21.0%	21.3%
Strongly disagree	2,745	69.7%	68.9%
Total valid	3,939	100.0%	100.0%
(Don't know/Not sure)	153		
(No answer/Refused)	11		
Total missing	164		
Total N	4,103	3,939	2,604

Table Q17c.2. Cross-tabulation by Visitation (weighted national data, recent visitors/non-visitors)

Response	Visitor	Non-visitor
Strongly agree	0.6%	4.3%
Somewhat agree	2.1%	5.8%
Neither	2.4%	4.0%
Somewhat disagree	18.3%	24.2%
Strongly disagree	76.7%	61.8%
Total	100.0%	100.0%
Valid weighted N	1,252	1,353

Chi-square test: p<.001

Table Q17c.3. Cross-tabulation by Region (weighted regional data, general public)

Response	AKR	PWR	IMR	MWR	SER	NER	NCR
Strongly agree	2.3%	3.2%	3.3%	2.7%	3.2%	1.8%	2.2%
Somewhat agree	3.0%	5.9%	4.7%	3.2%	4.7%	3.5%	2.9%
Neither	4.0%	3.6%	1.9%	2.4%	3.5%	4.1%	3.2%
Somewhat disagree	19.3%	18.5%	24.1%	20.7%	22.4%	23.9%	22.1%
Strongly disagree	71.5%	68.8%	65.9%	71.0%	66.2%	66.8%	69.6%
Total	100.0%	100.0%	100.0%	100.0%	100.0%	100.0%	100.0%
Valid weighted N	350	363	406	448	373	409	275

Chi-square test: p>.2

Q17d. [In random order] **"It takes too long to get to any National Park System units from my home."**

Table Q17d.1. Frequency Distribution (national data, general public)

Response	Unweighted Frequency	Unweighted Percent	Weighted Percent
Strongly agree	640	16.0%	17.3%
Somewhat agree	846	21.2%	24.8%
Neither agree nor disagree	177	4.4%	4.8%
Somewhat disagree	844	21.1%	22.8%
Strongly disagree	1,489	37.3%	30.2%
Total valid	3,996	100.0%	100.0%
(Don't know/Not sure)	97		
(No answer/Refused)	10		
Total missing	107		
Total N	4,103	3,996	2,642

Table Q17d.2. Cross-tabulation by Visitation (weighted national data, recent visitors/non-visitors)

Response	Visitor	Non-visitor
Strongly agree	11.0%	23.0%
Somewhat agree	23.6%	26.0%
Neither	4.4%	5.2%
Somewhat disagree	22.8%	22.9%
Strongly disagree	38.2%	23.0%
Total	100.0%	100.0%
Valid weighted N	1,255	1,387

Chi-square test: p<.001

Table Q17d.3. Cross-tabulation by Region (weighted regional data, general public)

Response	AKR	PWR	IMR	MWR	SER	NER	NCR
Strongly agree	24.0%	13.4%	21.4%	21.1%	21.5%	14.2%	5.9%
Somewhat agree	21.1%	24.3%	25.8%	29.3%	21.7%	20.6%	9.5%
Neither	2.8%	6.4%	4.8%	4.9%	2.7%	5.2%	3.2%
Somewhat disagree	17.9%	22.2%	19.8%	23.3%	22.3%	24.8%	14.0%
Strongly disagree	34.2%	33.7%	28.2%	21.4%	31.8%	35.3%	67.4%
Total	100.0%	100.0%	100.0%	100.0%	100.0%	100.0%	100.0%
Valid weighted N	354	370	415	454	374	416	279

Chi-square test: p<.001

Q17e. [In random order] "**National Park System units are too crowded.**"

Table Q17e.1. Frequency Distribution (national data, general public)

Response	Unweighted Frequency	Unweighted Percent	Weighted Percent
Strongly agree	321	8.4%	8.0%
Somewhat agree	848	22. 3%	20.0%
Neither agree nor disagree	365	9.6%	10.3%
Somewhat disagree	1,211	31.9%	32.5%
Strongly disagree	1,054	27.7%	29.1%
Total valid	3,799	100.0%	100.0%
(Don't know/Not sure)	292		
(No answer/Refused)	12		
Total missing	304		
Total N	4,103	3,799	2,522

Table Q17e.2. Cross-tabulation by Visitation (weighted national data, recent visitors/non-visitors)

Response	Visitor	Non-visitor
Strongly agree	5.9%	10.1%
Somewhat agree	21.7%	18.3%
Neither	10.2%	10.5%
Somewhat disagree	31.7%	33.3%
Strongly disagree	30.5%	27.9%
Total	100.0%	100.0%
Valid weighted N	1,244	1,279

Chi-square test: p<.01

Table Q17e.3. Cross-tabulation by Region (weighted regional data, general public)

Response	AKR	PWR	IMR	MWR	SER	NER	NCR
Strongly agree	10.5%	13.2%	9.4%	6.6%	7.3%	7.0%	10.7%
Somewhat agree	19.8%	23.2%	25.4%	19.4%	14.6%	20.8%	21.0%
Neither	10.9%	9.9%	10.2%	10.5%	8.6%	10.3%	6.5%
Somewhat disagree	30.1%	28.2%	25.9%	35.7%	34.3%	34.0%	31.1%
Strongly disagree	28.8%	25.4%	29.1%	27.9%	35.2%	27.9%	30.7%
Total	100.0%	100.0%	100.0%	100.0%	100.0%	100.0%	100.0%
Valid weighted N	338	357	393	431	358	390	277

Chi-square test: p<.01

Q17f. [In random order] **"It is difficult to find a parking space within National Park System units."**

Table Q17f.1. Frequency Distribution (national data, general public)

Response	Unweighted Frequency	Unweighted Percent	Weighted Percent
Strongly agree	367	9.9%	9.0%
Somewhat agree	619	16.8%	16.1%
Neither agree nor disagree	333	9.0%	10.1%
Somewhat disagree	1,029	27.9%	27.7%
Strongly disagree	1,344	36.4%	37.2%
Total valid	3,692	100.0%	100.0%
(Don't know/Not sure)	399		
(No answer/Refused)	12		
Total missing	411		
Total N	4,103	3,692	2,452

Table Q17f.2. Cross-tabulation by Visitation (weighted national data, recent visitors/non-visitors)

Response	Visitor	Non-visitor
Strongly agree	7.3%	10.7%
Somewhat agree	17.0%	15.3%
Neither	7.0%	13.1%
Somewhat disagree	28.4%	27.0%
Strongly disagree	40.4%	33.9%
Total	100.0%	100.0%
Valid weighted N	1,228	1,223

Chi-square test: p<.001

Table Q17f.3. Cross-tabulation by Region (weighted regional data, general public)

Response	AKR	PWR	IMR	MWR	SER	NER	NCR
Strongly agree	7.0%	12.8%	11.8%	5.4%	10.1%	9.7%	24.7%
Somewhat agree	19.7%	16.2%	17.6%	12.6%	12.8%	22.8%	14.5%
Neither	9.3%	9.1%	9.5%	10.2%	10.0%	9.7%	6.7%
Somewhat disagree	26.9%	28.4%	26.6%	27.6%	30.4%	24.3%	23.9%
Strongly disagree	37.2%	33.4%	34.5%	44.2%	36.7%	33.5%	30.1%
Total	100.0%	100.0%	100.0%	100.0%	100.0%	100.0%	100.0%
Valid weighted N	331	352	383	420	343	377	263

Chi-square test: p<.001

Q17g. [In random order] "**National Park System units are not accessible to persons with physical disabilities.**"

Table Q17g.1. Frequency Distribution (national data, general public)

Response	Unweighted Frequency	Unweighted Percent	Weighted Percent
Strongly agree	170	5.1%	4.5%
Somewhat agree	355	10.6%	11.5%
Neither agree nor disagree	433	12.9%	13.9%
Somewhat disagree	1,007	29.9%	28.2%
Strongly disagree	1,398	41.6%	42.0%
Total valid	3,363	100.0%	100.0%
(Don't know/Not sure)	709		
(No answer/Refused)	31		
Total missing	740		
Total N	4,103	3,363	2,267

Table Q17g.2. Cross-tabulation by Visitation (weighted national data, recent visitors/non-visitors)

Response	Visitor	Non-visitor
Strongly agree	3.2%	5.7%
Somewhat agree	11.0%	12.0%
Neither	12.5%	15.2%
Somewhat disagree	29.7%	26.7%
Strongly disagree	43.5%	40.5%
Total	100.0%	100.0%
Valid weighted N	1,105	1,162

Chi-square test: p<.01

Table Q17g.3. Cross-tabulation by Region (weighted regional data, general public)

Response	AKR	PWR	IMR	MWR	SER	NER	NCR
Strongly agree	6.9%	5.2%	6.6%	4.3%	6.4%	3.7%	5.3%
Somewhat agree	8.1%	13.2%	13.2%	10.2%	14.7%	10.5%	10.5%
Neither	13.7%	15.3%	13.9%	13.1%	11.1%	15.4%	10.8%
Somewhat disagree	32.2%	25.8%	24.1%	27.6%	29.8%	29.2%	28.7%
Strongly disagree	39.1%	40.5%	42.2%	44.8%	38.0%	41.2%	44.7%
Total	100.0%	100.0%	100.0%	100.0%	100.0%	100.0%	100.0%
Valid weighted N	309	321	351	382	336	339	237

Chi-square test: p>.2

Q17h. [In random order] **"I just don't know that much about National Park System units."**

Table Q17h.1. Frequency Distribution (national data, general public)

Response	Unweighted Frequency	Unweighted Percent	Weighted Percent
Strongly agree	724	18.0%	20.6%
Somewhat agree	935	23.2%	25.0%
Neither agree nor disagree	240	6.0%	6.3%
Somewhat disagree	911	22.6%	22.2%
Strongly disagree	1,221	30.3%	25.9%
Total valid	4,031	100.0%	100.0%
(Don't know/Not sure)	64		
(No answer/Refused)	8		
Total missing	72		
Total N	4,103	4,031	2,665

Table Q17h.2. Cross-tabulation by Visitation (weighted national data, recent visitors/non-visitors)

Response	Visitor	Non-visitor
Strongly agree	8.0%	31.8%
Somewhat agree	21.7%	28.0%
Neither	7.1%	5.6%
Somewhat disagree	28.3%	16.8%
Strongly disagree	34.9%	17.9%
Total	100.0%	100.0%
Valid weighted N	1,251	1,413

Chi-square test: p<.001

Table Q17h.3. Cross-tabulation by Region (weighted regional data, general public)

Response	AKR	PWR	IMR	MWR	SER	NER	NCR
Strongly agree	14.5%	18.3%	19.8%	19.7%	25.1%	20.8%	15.9%
Somewhat agree	19.3%	24.0%	24.2%	25.5%	25.2%	28.5%	15.6%
Neither	5.2%	5.1%	8.1%	6.9%	5.0%	6.3%	4.8%
Somewhat disagree	24.3%	20.9%	21.7%	23.2%	19.6%	21.5%	28.9%
Strongly disagree	36.6%	31.6%	26.3%	24.7%	25.2%	22.9%	34.8%
Total	100.0%	100.0%	100.0%	100.0%	100.0%	100.0%	100.0%
Valid weighted N	359	367	415	455	384	420	276

Chi-square test: p<.001

Q17i. [In random order] "**Reservations at National Park System units have to be made too far in advance.**"

Table Q17i.1. Frequency Distribution (national data, general public)

Response	Unweighted Frequency	Unweighted Percent	Weighted Percent
Strongly agree	502	15.3%	13.8%
Somewhat agree	737	22.4%	21.3%
Neither agree nor disagree	436	13.3%	13.4%
Somewhat disagree	831	25.3%	27.1%
Strongly disagree	779	23.7%	24.4%
Total valid	3,285	100.0%	100.0%
(Don't know/Not sure)	796		
(No answer/Refused)	22		
Total missing	818		
Total N	4,103	3,285	2,226

Table Q17i.2. Cross-tabulation by Visitation (weighted national data, recent visitors/non-visitors)

Response	Visitor	Non-visitor
Strongly agree	12.9%	14.7%
Somewhat agree	22.8%	19.8%
Neither	12.6%	14.2%
Somewhat disagree	27.5%	26.6%
Strongly disagree	24.1%	24.7%
Total	100.0%	100.0%
Valid weighted N	1,115	1,110

Chi-square test: p>.2

Table Q17i.3. Cross-tabulation by Region (weighted regional data, general public)

Response	AKR	PWR	IMR	MWR	SER	NER	NCR
Strongly agree	19.8%	23.5%	16.1%	12.6%	14.2%	8.2%	11.4%
Somewhat agree	24.6%	25.0%	22.8%	20.4%	19.3%	20.3%	12.6%
Neither	13.4%	11.9%	13.3%	15.1%	10.0%	16.1%	11.7%
Somewhat disagree	23.4%	22.4%	26.2%	26.0%	29.5%	29.6%	31.0%
Strongly disagree	18.8%	17.2%	21.6%	25.8%	27.0%	25.8%	33.2%
Total	100.0%	100.0%	100.0%	100.0%	100.0%	100.0%	100.0%
Valid weighted N	303	319	352	375	318	336	232

Chi-square test: p<.001

Q17j. [In random order] **"National Park Service employees give poor service to visitors."**

Table Q17j.1. Frequency Distribution (national data, general public)

Response	Unweighted Frequency	Unweighted Percent	Weighted Percent
Strongly agree	80	2.1%	1.8%
Somewhat agree	144	3.8%	4.7%
Neither agree nor disagree	196	5.2%	6.4%
Somewhat disagree	784	20.7%	20.9%
Strongly disagree	2,579	68.2%	66.3%
Total valid	3,783	100.0%	100.0%
(Don't know/Not sure)	303		
(No answer/Refused)	17		
Total missing	320		
Total N	4,103	3,783	2,490

Table Q17j.2. Cross-tabulation by Visitation (weighted national data, recent visitors/non-visitors)

Response	Visitor	Non-visitor
Strongly agree	1.0%	2.5%
Somewhat agree	3.5%	5.9%
Neither	4.1%	8.6%
Somewhat disagree	18.8%	22.9%
Strongly disagree	72.6%	60.0%
Total	100.0%	100.0%
Valid weighted N	1,244	1,246

Chi-square test: p<.001

Table Q17j.3. Cross-tabulation by Region (weighted regional data, general public)

Response	AKR	PWR	IMR	MWR	SER	NER	NCR
Strongly agree	2.9%	1.9%	1.9%	1.6%	3.3%	1.0%	2.6%
Somewhat agree	5.4%	3.4%	6.4%	3.2%	4.9%	6.4%	4.3%
Neither	4.7%	6.6%	6.8%	7.4%	5.2%	6.4%	5.7%
Somewhat disagree	22.7%	20.0%	19.9%	24.0%	18.8%	20.5%	25.0%
Strongly disagree	64.3%	68.3%	65.0%	63.9%	67.8%	65.7%	62.4%
Total	100.0%	100.0%	100.0%	100.0%	100.0%	100.0%	100.0%
Valid weighted N	331	356	393	423	350	388	268

Chi-square test: p>.2

Q17k. [In random order] **"National Park System units are unpleasant places for me to be."**

Table Q17k.1. Frequency Distribution (national data, general public)

Response	Unweighted Frequency	Unweighted Percent	Weighted Percent
Strongly agree	86	2.2%	2.7%
Somewhat agree	117	3.0%	3.0%
Neither agree nor disagree	76	1.9%	1.9%
Somewhat disagree	486	12.3%	14.4%
Strongly disagree	3,198	80.7%	77.9%
Total valid	3,963	100.0%	100.0%
(Don't know/Not sure)	125		
(No answer/Refused)	15		
Total missing	140		
Total N	4,103	3,963	2,612

Table Q17k.2. Cross-tabulation by Visitation (weighted national data, recent visitors/non-visitors)

Response	Visitor	Non-visitor
Strongly agree	1.4%	4.0%
Somewhat agree	1.2%	4.7%
Neither	0.9%	2.9%
Somewhat disagree	10.4%	18.1%
Strongly disagree	86.1%	70.3%
Total	100.0%	100.0%
Valid weighted N	1,256	1,356

Chi-square test: p<.001

Table Q17k.3. Cross-tabulation by Region (weighted regional data, general public)

Response	AKR	PWR	IMR	MWR	SER	NER	NCR
Strongly agree	1.7%	6.5%	2.8%	1.2%	3.7%	1.2%	2.5%
Somewhat agree	3.5%	3.4%	4.0%	2.9%	3.5%	1.7%	3.1%
Neither	2.6%	1.7%	1.9%	2.4%	2.4%	1.3%	1.5%
Somewhat disagree	11.4%	10.0%	17.1%	14.6%	14.0%	15.7%	12.7%
Strongly disagree	80.8%	78.4%	74.2%	78.9%	76.5%	80.1%	80.2%
Total	100.0%	100.0%	100.0%	100.0%	100.0%	100.0%	100.0%
Valid weighted N	349	367	408	442	372	413	278

Chi-square test: p<.01

Q17l. [In random order] **"There isn't enough information available about what to do once inside a National Park System unit."**

Table Q17l.1. Frequency Distribution (national data, general public)

Response	Unweighted Frequency	Unweighted Percent	Weighted Percent
Strongly agree	314	8.2%	10.0%
Somewhat agree	417	10.9%	12.7%
Neither agree nor disagree	199	5.2%	5.2%
Somewhat disagree	965	25.2%	25.1%
Strongly disagree	1,938	50.6%	47.0%
Total valid	3,833	100.0%	100.0%
(Don't know/Not sure)	257		
(No answer/Refused)	13		
Total missing	270		
Total N	4,103	3,833	2,542

Table Q17l.2. Cross-tabulation by Visitation (weighted national data, recent visitors/non-visitors)

Response	Visitor	Non-visitor
Strongly agree	6.5%	13.3%
Somewhat agree	10.6%	14.7%
Neither	3.7%	6.7%
Somewhat disagree	23.5%	26.5%
Strongly disagree	55.7%	38.7%
Total	100.0%	100.0%
Valid weighted N	1,238	1,303

Chi-square test: p<.001

Table Q17l.3. Cross-tabulation by Region (weighted regional data, general public)

Response	AKR	PWR	IMR	MWR	SER	NER	NCR
Strongly agree	6.4%	10.5%	10.7%	9.5%	11.7%	8.7%	9.6%
Somewhat agree	9.4%	11.1%	12.0%	14.4%	15.3%	11.2%	9.3%
Neither	5.3%	4.7%	4.7%	6.1%	5.2%	4.2%	5.3%
Somewhat disagree	25.0%	24.8%	28.3%	24.1%	23.1%	25.7%	22.8%
Strongly disagree	53.9%	48.9%	44.3%	45.9%	44.8%	50.2%	53.0%
Total	100.0%	100.0%	100.0%	100.0%	100.0%	100.0%	100.0%
Valid weighted N	340	352	400	436	360	399	272

Chi-square test: p>.2

Q17m. [In random order] "**I prefer to spend my free time doing electronic activities, like watching videos, enjoying computer games, or surfing the Internet.**"

Table Q17m.1. Frequency Distribution (national data, general public)

Response	Unweighted Frequency	Unweighted Percent	Weighted Percent
Strongly agree	213	5.2%	6.4%
Somewhat agree	368	9.0%	11.0%
Neither agree nor disagree	182	4.5%	5.5%
Somewhat disagree	599	14.7%	17.1%
Strongly disagree	2,715	66.6%	60.0%
Total valid	4,077	100.0%	100.0%
(Don't know/Not sure)	13		
(No answer/Refused)	13		
Total missing	26		
Total N	4,103	4,077	2,695

Table Q17m.2. Cross-tabulation by Visitation (weighted national data, recent visitors/non-visitors)

Response	Visitor	Non-visitor
Strongly agree	3.4%	9.2%
Somewhat agree	9.1%	12.7%
Neither	5.0%	5.8%
Somewhat disagree	15.0%	18.9%
Strongly disagree	67.5%	53.4%
Total	100.0%	100.0%
Valid weighted N	1,256	1,437

Chi-square test: p<.001

Table Q17m.3. Cross-tabulation by Region (weighted regional data, general public)

Response	AKR	PWR	IMR	MWR	SER	NER	NCR
Strongly agree	3.6%	7.7%	8.1%	4.1%	6.1%	8.0%	7.5%
Somewhat agree	6.7%	13.0%	11.0%	9.8%	10.7%	10.5%	12.3%
Neither	4.7%	5.4%	6.3%	4.4%	5.2%	6.9%	4.2%
Somewhat disagree	11.2%	14.9%	13.6%	17.1%	16.3%	20.1%	18.1%
Strongly disagree	73.8%	59.0%	61.0%	64.7%	61.6%	54.6%	57.9%
Total	100.0%	100.0%	100.0%	100.0%	100.0%	100.0%	100.0%
Valid weighted N	359	374	420	461	388	424	282

Chi-square test: p<.01

Q18. In your opinion, what is the ONE most important thing the National Park Service can do to encourage you to visit units of the National Park System?

(Do NOT read choices; code the ONE most important thing. Use "Other, specify" if respondent names anything other than the choices shown.)

Table Q18.1. Frequency Distribution (national data, general public)

Response	Unweighted Frequency	Unweighted Percent	Weighted Percent
Nothing, no suggestion, no ideas	532	14.5%	13.5%
Keep up the current approach, good job as is	251	6.8%	6.1%
Advertise, publicize, provide more information	1,303	35.5%	41.5%
Lower the fees and/or make admission free	204	5.6%	5.9%
Provide more parking	34	0.9%	0.9%
Make units easier and/or cheaper to get to, closer in proximity	179	4.9%	4.7%
Other	1,163	31.7%	27.3%
Total valid	3,666	100.0%	100.0%
(Don't know/Not sure)	407		
(No answer/Refused)	30		
Total missing	437		
Total N	4,103	3,666	2,400

Table Q18.2. Cross-tabulation by Visitation (weighted national data, recent visitors/non-visitors)

Response	Visitor	Non-visitor
Nothing, no suggestion, no ideas	12.0%	15.0%
Keep up the current approach, good job as is	7.7%	4.6%
Advertise, publicize, provide more information	38.3%	44.5%
Lower the fees and/or make admission free	5.0%	6.8%
Provide more parking	1.4%	0.5%
Make units easier and/or cheaper to get to, closer in proximity	4.5%	4.9%
Other	31.2%	23.8%
Total	100.0%	100.0%
Valid weighted N	1,158	1,242

Chi-square test: p<.001

Table Q18.3. Cross-tabulation by Region (weighted regional data, general public)

Response	AKR	PWR	IMR	MWR	SER	NER	NCR
Nothing, no suggestion, no ideas	15.9%	12.6%	13.6%	13.3%	17.3%	12.6%	9.6%
Keep up the current approach, good job as is	8.4%	9.1%	4.7%	5.5%	6.0%	6.4%	4.8%
Advertise, publicize, provide more information	23.3%	33.3%	37.1%	40.4%	44.3%	43.6%	40.0%
Lower the fees and/or make admission free	5.0%	5.6%	9.1%	6.5%	5.3%	5.6%	3.1%
Provide more parking	1.1%	1.2%	2.0%	0.2%	0.4%	1.5%	2.5%
Make units easier and/or cheaper to get to, closer in proximity	6.0%	4.0%	5.2%	7.5%	3.2%	4.2%	1.4%
Other	40.3%	34.2%	28.2%	26.6%	23.5%	26.1%	38.7%
Total	100.0%	100.0%	100.0%	100.0%	100.0%	100.0%	100.0%
Valid weighted N	326	339	372	414	340	376	258

Chi-square test: $p < .001$

Q19. [For Visitors in random subset A] **During your last visit to** [Unit Name] **did you stay overnight there, either in the park itself, in a neighboring community, or both?**

Table Q19. Frequency Distribution (national data, recent visitors)

Response	Unweighted Frequency	Unweighted Percent	Weighted Percent
No, did not stay overnight	437	40.3%	39.1%
Stayed in park only	143	13.2%	13.2%
Stayed in neighboring community only	445	41.0%	43.2%
Both in park and neighboring community	60	5.5%	4.5%
Total valid	1,085	100.0%	100.0%
(Don't know/Not sure)	7		
(No Answer/Refused)	1		
(Not asked, random split)	1,082		
Total missing	1,090		
Total N	2,175	1,085	621

Q20. [For Visitors in random subset A who said In the Park on Q19] **While you were in the park, did you stay in any of the following?**

(Read choices one at a time, and mark ALL that apply.)

Table Q20. Multiple Response Frequencies (national data, recent visitors who stayed in the park)

Response	Unweighted Frequency	Unweighted Percent	Weighted Percent
A lodge or hotel within the park	55	27.2%	22.3%
A campground inside the park for tents or RVs	119	58.9%	62.7%
Overnight camping reached by backpack, horseback, boat, or aircraft	35	17.3%	16.4%
Any other park lodging	10	5.0%	8.0%
(None of the above -- stayed in vehicle, kept moving, did not sleep, etc.)	9	4.5%	2.3%
(Don't know/Not sure)	0		
(No answer/Refused)	1		
(Not asked/Not applicable)	1,972		
Total missing	1,973		
Total N	2,175	202	109

This is a mark-all-that-apply question; percentages total more than 100.

Q21. [For Visitors in random subset A who said In the Community on Q19] **While you were in the community, did you stay in any of these?**

(Read choices one at a time, and mark ALL that apply.)

Table Q21. Multiple Response Frequencies (national data, recent visitors who stayed in the community)

Response	Unweighted Frequency	Unweighted Percent	Weighted Percent
A hotel, motel, inn, or bed & breakfast	296	59.7%	68.0%
A neighboring campground for tents or RVs	54	10.9%	9.1%
With family or friends	120	24.2%	19.9%
Any other community lodging	41	8.3%	9.2%
(None of the above--stayed in vehicle, kept moving, did not sleep, etc.)	35	7.1%	3.9%
(Don't know/Not sure)	6		
(No answer/Refused)	3		
(Not asked/Not applicable)	1,670		
Total missing	1,679		
Total N	2,175	496	294

This is a mark-all-that-apply question; percentages total more than 100.

[Note to the reader: Question 22 was eliminated during pretesting.]

Q23. [For random subset B] **Before this survey, were you aware of any of the following ways that people can help national parks?**

Q23a. [In random order] **Volunteering time to do needed jobs in parks.**

(As needed: Were you aware of this way to help national parks?)

Table Q23a.1. Frequency Distribution (national data, general public)

Response	Unweighted Frequency	Unweighted Percent	Weighted Percent
Yes (aware of this)	1,126	57.1%	54.3%
No	847	42.9%	45.7%
Total valid	1,973	100.0%	100.0%
(Don't know/Not sure)	12		
(No answer/Refused)	0		
(Not asked, random split)	2,118		
Total missing	2,130		
Total N	4,103	1,973	1,296

Table Q23a.2. Cross-tabulation by Visitation (weighted national data, recent visitors/non-visitors)

Response	Visitor	Non-visitor
Yes (aware of this)	62.0%	46.8%
No	38.0%	53.2%
Total	100.0%	100.0%
Valid weighted N	635	662

Chi-square test: p<.001

Q23b. [In random order] **Making a monetary donation.**

Table Q23b.1. Frequency Distribution (national data, general public)

Response	Unweighted Frequency	Unweighted Percent	Weighted Percent
Yes (aware of this)	1,307	66.3%	66.1%
No	665	33.7%	33.9%
Total valid	1,972	100.0%	100.0%
(Don't know/Not sure)	11		
(No answer/Refused)	2		
(Not asked, random split)	2,118		
Total missing	2,131		
Total N	4,103	1,972	1,293

Table Q23b.2. Cross-tabulation by Visitation (weighted national data, recent visitors/non-visitors)

Response	Visitor	Non-visitor
Yes (aware of this)	75.0%	57.5%
No	25.0%	42.5%
Total	100.0%	100.0%
Valid weighted N	636	657

Chi-square test: p<.001

Q23c. [In random order] **Donating things to parks, such as equipment or historical artifacts.**

Table Q23c.1. Frequency Distribution (national data, general public)

Response	Unweighted Frequency	Unweighted Percent	Weighted Percent
Yes (aware of this)	761	38.6%	36.9%
No	1,210	61.4%	63.1%
Total valid	1,971	100.0%	100.0%
(Don't know/Not sure)	13		
(No answer/Refused)	1		
(Not asked, random split)	2,118		
Total missing	2,132		
Total N	4,103	1,971	1,291

Table Q23c.2. Cross-tabulation by Visitation (weighted national data, recent visitors/non-visitors)

Response	Visitor	Non-visitor
Yes (aware of this)	40.8%	33.1%
No	59.2%	66.9%
Total	100.0%	100.0%
Valid weighted N	636	656

Chi-square test: p<.01

Q23d. [In random order] **Joining a park friends association.**

Table Q23d.1. Frequency Distribution (national data, general public)

Response	Unweighted Frequency	Unweighted Percent	Weighted Percent
Yes (aware of this)	762	38.8%	35.7%
No	1,200	61.2%	64.3%
Total valid	1,962	100.0%	100.0%
(Don't know/Not sure)	22		
(No answer/Refused)	1		
(Not asked, random split)	2,118		
Total missing	2,141		
Total N	4,103	1,962	1,287

Table Q23d.2. Cross-tabulation by Visitation (weighted national data, recent visitors/non-visitors)

Response	Visitor	Non-visitor
Yes (aware of this)	42.9%	28.7%
No	57.1%	71.3%
Total	100.0%	100.0%
Valid weighted N	629	658

Chi-square test: p<.001

Q24. [For those in random subset B aware of at least one of Q23a-d] **Have you actually helped a park system unit in any of these ways?**

(Do NOT read choices; check ALL that respondent reports.)

Table Q24.1. Multiple Response Frequencies (national data, general public aware of ways to help)

Response	Unweighted Frequency	Unweighted Percent	Weighted Percent
Donated money	269	17.8%	16.9%
Donated things	40	2.6%	2.3%
Joined a friends association	48	3.2%	2.3%
Volunteered time	170	11.3%	10.4%
Helped some other way	63	4.2%	4.4%
(None of the above, has not helped)	1,021	67.6%	68.8%
(Don't know/Not sure)	19		
(No answer/Refused)	22		
(Not asked, aware of none)	433		
(Not asked, random split)	2,118		
Total missing	2,592		
Total N	4,103	1,511	979

This is a mark-all-that-apply question; percentages total more than 100.

Table Q24.2. Multiple Response Frequencies by Visitation (weighted national data, recent visitors/non-visitors aware of ways to help)

Response	Visitor	Non-visitor
Donated money	23.5%	9.0%
Donated things	2.9%	1.6%
Joined a friends association	3.1%	1.4%
Volunteered time	12.5%	7.9%
Helped some other way	4.9%	3.8%
(None of the above, has not helped)	60.6%	78.6%
Valid weighted N	663	316

This is a mark-all-that-apply question; percentages total more than 100 within visitor status.

Q25. [For random subset B] **Now, please think about the SOUNDS in a large national park like Yellowstone, Grand Canyon, or Great Smoky Mountains. These parks have lots of natural sounds, like birds singing, water flowing in rivers, and sounds of wildlife such as elk or frogs. These parks may also have sounds from vehicles and aircraft or from construction and maintenance equipment.**

We'd like to know how important it is to hear the SOUNDS OF NATURE for enjoying an experience in the wild or undeveloped areas of a large national park. For you personally, is hearing the sounds of nature ...

(Read choices; mark ONE response.)

Table Q25.1. Frequency Distribution (national data, general public)

Response	Unweighted Frequency	Unweighted Percent	Weighted Percent
Not important at all	19	1.0%	0.9%
Somewhat unimportant	27	1.4%	1.2%
Neither important nor unimportant	64	3.3%	3.5%
Somewhat important	389	19.8%	19.4%
Very important	1,466	74.6%	74.9%
Total valid	1,965	100.0%	100.0%
(Don't know/Not sure)	10		
(No answer/Refused)	10		
(Not asked, random split)	2,118		
Total missing	2,138		
Total N	4,103	1,965	1,294

Table Q25.2. Cross-tabulation by Visitation (weighted national data, recent visitors/non-visitors)

Response	Visitor	Non-visitor
Not important at all	1.1%	0.7%
Somewhat unimportant	1.2%	1.1%
Neither important nor unimportant	3.9%	3.2%
Somewhat important	19.9%	19.0%
Very important	73.8%	76.0%
Total	100.0%	100.0%
Valid weighted N	634	659

Chi-square test: p>.2

Q26. [For random subset B] **How much do you agree or disagree with the following statement?**

"I should be able to go to a national park and not hear mechanized sounds like engine noise and cell phones when I am in wild or undeveloped areas." Do you …

(Read choices; mark ONE response.)

Table Q26.1. Frequency Distribution (national data, general public)

Response	Unweighted Frequency	Unweighted Percent	Weighted Percent
Strongly agree	967	49.3%	47.1%
Somewhat agree	502	25.6%	28.8%
Neither agree nor disagree	150	7.6%	8.4%
Somewhat disagree	215	11.0%	10.1%
Strongly disagree	129	6.6%	5.7%
Total valid	1,963	100.0%	100.0%
(Don't know/Not sure)	14		
(No answer/Refused)	8		
(Not asked, random split)	2,118		
Total missing	2,140		
Total N	4,103	1,963	1,293

Table Q26.2. Cross-tabulation by Visitation (weighted national data, recent visitors/non-visitors)

Response	Visitor	Non-visitor
Strongly agree	48.9%	45.4%
Somewhat agree	29.4%	28.2%
Neither agree nor disagree	6.7%	10.0%
Somewhat disagree	9.8%	10.5%
Strongly disagree	5.3%	6.0%
Total	100.0%	100.0%
Valid weighted N	637	658

Chi-square test: p>.2

Q27. [For random subset B] **Next, think about the sounds in a HISTORICAL park, like Gettysburg, Valley Forge, or the cliff dwellings at Mesa Verde. Parks like these honor historic events or early cultures. The exhibits and programs there may have cultural and historical sounds, such as musket fire, folk songs, or Native American music.**

We'd like to know how important it is to hear CULTURAL AND HISTORICAL SOUNDS like that for enjoying an experience in one of those parks. For you personally, is hearing cultural and historical sounds ...

(Read choices; mark ONE response.)

Table Q27.1. Frequency Distribution (national data, general public)

Response	Unweighted Frequency	Unweighted Percent	Weighted Percent
Not important at all	76	3.9%	2.6%
Somewhat unimportant	79	4.0%	4.0%
Neither important nor unimportant	112	5.7%	5.4%
Somewhat important	597	30.4%	30.3%
Very important	1,101	56.0%	57.7%
Total valid	1,965	100.0%	100.0%
(Don't know/Not sure)	13		
(No answer/Refused)	7		
(Not asked, random split)	2,118		
Total missing	2,138		
Total N	4,103	1,965	1,297

Table Q27.2. Cross-tabulation by Visitation (weighted national data, recent visitors/non-visitors)

Response	Visitor	Non-visitor
Not important at all	2.1%	3.0%
Somewhat unimportant	4.7%	3.3%
Neither important nor unimportant	5.8%	4.9%
Somewhat important	31.8%	28.9%
Very important	55.6%	59.8%
Total	100.0%	100.0%
Valid weighted N	635	661

Chi-square test: p>.2

Q28. [For random subset B] **The large national parks like Yellowstone, Grand Canyon, and Great Smoky Mountains are known for their natural resources. For example, they have interesting plants and animals, remote areas and wilderness, lakes or rivers, and starry night skies. I'm going to read you some statements about these parks and ask you how much you personally agree or disagree with each statement.**

Q28a. [In random order] "**Plants that do not occur naturally in these parks should be removed.**"

(As needed: Would you say you "strongly agree," "somewhat agree," "neither agree or disagree," "somewhat disagree," or "strongly disagree" with this statement for large national parks? Plants include trees, flowers, grasses, etc.)

Table Q28a.1. Frequency Distribution (national data, general public)

Response	Unweighted Frequency	Unweighted Percent	Weighted Percent
Strongly agree	511	27.1%	24.6%
Somewhat agree	508	26.9%	26.7%
Neither agree nor disagree	200	10.6%	10.3%
Somewhat disagree	374	19.8%	20.9%
Strongly disagree	295	15.6%	17.4%
Total valid	1,888	100.0%	100.0%
(Don't know/Not sure)	86		
(No answer/Refused)	11		
(Not asked, random split)	2,118		
Total missing	2,215		
Total N	4,103	1,888	1,251

Table Q28a.2. Cross-tabulation by Visitation (weighted national data, recent visitors/non-visitors)

Response	Visitor	Non-visitor
Strongly agree	26.2%	23.1%
Somewhat agree	26.8%	26.7%
Neither agree nor disagree	12.7%	7.9%
Somewhat disagree	22.0%	19.8%
Strongly disagree	12.2%	22.5%
Total	100.0%	100.0%
Valid weighted N	618	632

Chi-square test: p<.001

Q28b. [In random order] **"Animals that do not occur naturally in these parks should be removed."**

(As needed: ... Animals include wildlife, birds, fish, etc.)

Table Q28b.1. Frequency Distribution (national data, general public)

Response	Unweighted Frequency	Unweighted Percent	Weighted Percent
Strongly agree	422	22.4%	21.5%
Somewhat agree	476	25.3%	25.1%
Neither agree nor disagree	238	12.6%	12.2%
Somewhat disagree	396	21.0%	22.5%
Strongly disagree	353	18.7%	18.7%
Total valid	1,885	100.0%	100.0%
(Don't know/Not sure)	84		
(No answer/Refused)	16		
(Not asked, random split)	2,118		
Total missing	2,218		
Total N	4,103	1,885	1,257

Table Q28b.2. Cross-tabulation by Visitation (weighted national data, recent visitors/non-visitors)

Response	Visitor	Non-visitor
Strongly agree	18.1%	24.9%
Somewhat agree	25.1%	25.0%
Neither agree nor disagree	17.5%	7.0%
Somewhat disagree	23.9%	21.2%
Strongly disagree	15.4%	22.0%
Total	100.0%	100.0%
Valid weighted N	620	636

Chi-square test: p<.001

Q28c. [In random order] **"Animals that used to occur naturally in these parks should be brought back."**

(As needed: … Animals include wildlife, birds, fish, etc.)

Table Q28c.1. Frequency Distribution (national data, general public)

Response	Unweighted Frequency	Unweighted Percent	Weighted Percent
Strongly agree	1,066	54.9%	56.0%
Somewhat agree	593	30.5%	28.5%
Neither agree nor disagree	104	5.4%	5.5%
Somewhat disagree	88	4.5%	5.0%
Strongly disagree	92	4.7%	5.0%
Total valid	1,943	100.0%	100.0%
(Don't know/Not sure)	35		
(No answer/Refused)	7		
(Not asked, random split)	2,118		
Total missing	2,160		
Total N	4,103	1,943	1,278

Table Q28c.2. Cross-tabulation by Visitation (weighted national data, recent visitors/non-visitors)

Response	Visitor	Non-visitor
Strongly agree	54.3%	57.7%
Somewhat agree	32.5%	24.6%
Neither agree nor disagree	6.7%	4.4%
Somewhat disagree	4.0%	5.9%
Strongly disagree	2.6%	7.4%
Total	100.0%	100.0%
Valid weighted N	629	648

Chi-square test: p<.001

Q28d. [In random order] **"Aircraft flights should be limited over wild and undeveloped areas of these parks."**

Table Q28d.1. Frequency distribution (national data, general public)

Response	Unweighted Frequency	Unweighted Percent	Weighted Percent
Strongly agree	734	38.0%	38.6%
Somewhat agree	575	29.8%	28.5%
Neither agree nor disagree	166	8.6%	9.8%
Somewhat disagree	247	12.8%	12.3%
Strongly disagree	208	10.8%	10.9%
Total valid	1,930	100.0%	100.0%
(Don't know/Not sure)	49		
(No answer/Refused)	6		
(Not asked, random split)	2,118		
Total missing	2,173		
Total N	4,103	1,930	1,271

Table Q28d.2. Cross-tabulation by visitation (weighted national data, recent visitors/non-visitors)

Response	Visitor	Non-visitor
Strongly agree	38.1%	39.1%
Somewhat agree	29.1%	27.9%
Neither agree nor disagree	10.7%	8.9%
Somewhat disagree	13.1%	11.5%
Strongly disagree	9.0%	12.7%
Total	100.0%	100.0%
Valid weighted N	625	646

Chi-square test: p=.200

Q28e. [In random order] **"These national parks are places where there should be no air pollution from communities and industries."**

Table Q28e.1. Frequency Distribution (national data, general public)

Response	Unweighted Frequency	Unweighted Percent	Weighted Percent
Strongly agree	1,267	64.9%	67.0%
Somewhat agree	435	22.3%	21.4%
Neither agree nor disagree	84	4.3%	3.8%
Somewhat disagree	105	5.4%	5.3%
Strongly disagree	60	3.1%	2.5%
Total valid	1,951	100.0%	100.0%
(Don't know/Not sure)	22		
(No answer/Refused)	12		
(Not asked, random split)	2,118		
Total missing	2,152		
Total N	4,103	1,951	1,284

Table Q28e.2. Cross-tabulation by Visitation (weighted national data, recent visitors/non-visitors)

Response	Visitor	Non-visitor
Strongly agree	63.0%	70.9%
Somewhat agree	24.8%	18.1%
Neither agree nor disagree	4.1%	3.4%
Somewhat disagree	5.9%	4.8%
Strongly disagree	2.2%	2.8%
Total	100.0%	100.0%
Valid weighted N	634	651

Chi-square test: $p < .05$

80

Q28f. [In random order] "**These national parks are places I should be able to go and see the night sky without interference of artificial lights from nearby communities.**"

Table Q28f.1. Frequency Distribution (national data, general public)

Response	Unweighted Frequency	Unweighted Percent	Weighted Percent
Strongly agree	1,034	53.2%	55.1%
Somewhat agree	544	28.0%	27.6%
Neither agree nor disagree	110	5.7%	5.5%
Somewhat disagree	166	8.5%	7.8%
Strongly disagree	88	4.5%	3.9%
Total valid	1,942	100.0%	100.0%
(Don't know/Not sure)	33		
(No answer/Refused)	10		
(Not asked, random split)	2,118		
Total missing	2,161		
Total N	4,103	1,942	1,274

Table Q28f.2. Cross-tabulation by Visitation (weighted national data, recent visitors/non-visitors)

Response	Visitor	Non-visitor
Strongly agree	52.9%	57.3%
Somewhat agree	29.4%	25.9%
Neither agree nor disagree	6.1%	4.9%
Somewhat disagree	8.6%	7.1%
Strongly disagree	3.1%	4.7%
Total	100.0%	100.0%
Valid weighted N	630	643

Chi-square test: p=.180

Q28g. [In random order] "**These national parks are places where there should be no water pollution from communities, industries, and agriculture.**"

Table Q28g.1. Frequency Distribution (national data, general public)

Response	Unweighted Frequency	Unweighted Percent	Weighted Percent
Strongly agree	1,472	74.9%	76.8%
Somewhat agree	324	16.5%	14.7%
Neither agree nor disagree	53	2.7%	2.7%
Somewhat disagree	77	3.9%	3.8%
Strongly disagree	38	1.9%	2.0%
Total valid	1,964	100.0%	100.0%
(Don't know/Not sure)	16		
(No answer/Refused)	5		
(Not asked, random split)	2,118		
Total missing	2,139		
Total N	4,103	1,964	1,292

Table Q28g.2. Cross-tabulation by Visitation (weighted national data, recent visitors/non-visitors)

Response	Visitor	Non-visitor
Strongly agree	76.6%	77.0%
Somewhat agree	16.6%	12.8%
Neither agree nor disagree	2.2%	3.3%
Somewhat disagree	3.6%	4.0%
Strongly disagree	1.1%	2.8%
Total	100.0%	100.0%
Valid weighted N	636	657

Chi-square test: p<.05

Q28h. [In random order] **"Basic visitor facilities should be provided in these parks, such as roads, trails, restrooms, and water fountains."**

Table Q28h.1. Frequency Distribution (national data, general public)

Response	Unweighted Frequency	Unweighted Percent	Weighted Percent
Strongly agree	1,267	64.6%	64.7%
Somewhat agree	560	28.5%	28.1%
Neither agree nor disagree	45	2.3%	2.6%
Somewhat disagree	60	3.1%	2.5%
Strongly disagree	30	1.5%	2.1%
Total valid	1,962	100.0%	100.0%
(Don't know/Not sure)	18		
(No answer/Refused)	5		
(Not asked, random split)	2,118		
Total missing	2,141		
Total N	4,103	1,962	1,290

Table Q28h.2. Cross-tabulation by Visitation (weighted national data, recent visitors/non-visitors)

Response	Visitor	Non-visitor
Strongly agree	64.1%	65.2%
Somewhat agree	28.5%	27.8%
Neither agree nor disagree	3.1%	2.1%
Somewhat disagree	2.9%	2.2%
Strongly disagree	1.4%	2.7%
Total	100.0%	100.0%
Valid weighted N	635	657

Chi-square test: p>.2

Q28i. [In random order] **"Major visitor facilities should be provided in these parks, such as lodges, restaurants, and stores."**

Table Q28i.1. Frequency Distribution (national data, general public)

Response	Unweighted Frequency	Unweighted Percent	Weighted Percent
Strongly agree	486	24.9%	25.1%
Somewhat agree	711	36.5%	35.8%
Neither agree nor disagree	174	8.9%	8.8%
Somewhat disagree	355	18.2%	19.3%
Strongly disagree	222	11.4%	11.1%
Total valid	1,948	100.0%	100.0%
(Don't know/Not sure)	29		
(No answer/Refused)	8		
(Not asked, random split)	2,118		
Total missing	2,155		
Total N	4,103	1,948	1,282

Table Q28i.2. Cross-tabulation by Visitation (weighted national data, recent visitors/non-visitors)

Response	Visitor	Non-visitor
Strongly agree	22.1%	28.0%
Somewhat agree	36.4%	35.2%
Neither agree nor disagree	9.2%	8.4%
Somewhat disagree	22.4%	16.3%
Strongly disagree	10.0%	12.1%
Total	100.0%	100.0%
Valid weighted N	630	651

Chi-square test: $p < .05$

Q28j. [In random order] "**The number of private vehicles in these parks should be limited during the busiest periods.**"

Table Q28j.1. Frequency Distribution (national data, general public)

Response	Unweighted Frequency	Unweighted Percent	Weighted Percent
Strongly agree	782	40.4%	37.9%
Somewhat agree	665	34.4%	34.4%
Neither agree nor disagree	139	7.2%	7.4%
Somewhat disagree	198	10.2%	12.3%
Strongly disagree	150	7.8%	8.1%
Total valid	1,934	100.0%	100.0%
(Don't know/Not sure)	40		
(No answer/Refused)	11		
(Not asked, random split)	2,118		
Total missing	2,169		
Total N	4,103	1,934	1,269

Table Q28j.2. Cross-tabulation by Visitation (weighted national data, recent visitors/non-visitors)

Response	Visitor	Non-visitor
Strongly agree	39.5%	36.2%
Somewhat agree	35.9%	32.9%
Neither agree nor disagree	6.5%	8.3%
Somewhat disagree	12.4%	12.2%
Strongly disagree	5.7%	10.5%
Total	100.0%	100.0%
Valid weighted N	630	639

Chi-square test: p<.05

Q28k. [In random order] **"Jet-skiing and snowmobiling should be allowed in these parks."**

Table Q28k.1. Frequency Distribution (national data, general public)

Response	Unweighted Frequency	Unweighted Percent	Weighted Percent
Strongly agree	248	13.0%	11.8%
Somewhat agree	441	23.0%	24.0%
Neither agree nor disagree	173	9.0%	9.8%
Somewhat disagree	354	18.5%	19.2%
Strongly disagree	699	36.5%	35.1%
Total valid	1,915	100.0%	100.0%
(Don't know/Not sure)	59		
(No answer/Refused)	11		
(Not asked, random split)	2,118		
Total missing	2,188		
Total N	4,103	1,915	1,254

Table Q28k.2. Cross-tabulation by Visitation (weighted national data, recent visitors/non-visitors)

Response	Visitor	Non-visitor
Strongly agree	12.3%	11.3%
Somewhat agree	23.4%	24.6%
Neither agree nor disagree	9.0%	10.6%
Somewhat disagree	21.2%	17.2%
Strongly disagree	34.0%	36.2%
Total	100.0%	100.0%
Valid weighted N	623	630

Chi-square test: p>.2

D1a. **To finish, I need to ask you some questions so we can be sure our sample is representative.**

D1b. **We need to ask about calls you might receive on cell phones. Not counting your work-related calls, calls you don't answer, or out-going calls, when you personally take an in-coming call, is it ...**

(Read ONLY responses [in bold], but code [others] if volunteered.)

Table D1b.1. Frequency Distribution (national data, general public)

Response	Unweighted Frequency	Unweighted Percent	Weighted Percent
(Volunteered: Has access ONLY to cell phones)	16	0.4%	0.7%
Almost always on a cell phone	711	17.5%	29.9%
Usually on a cell phone	524	12.9%	14.7%
(Volunteered: On a cell phone about HALF the time)	40	1.0%	0.8%
Sometimes on a cell phone	1,328	32.7%	34.3%
Almost never on a cell phone	1,159	28.5%	15.9%
(Volunteered: Has NO access to a cell phone)	282	6.9%	3.5%
Total valid	4,060	100.0%	100.0%
(Don't know/Not sure)	12		
(No answer/Refused)	31		
Total missing	43		
Total N	4,103	4,060	2,680

Table D1b.2. Cross-tabulation by Visitation (weighted national data, general public)

Response	% Visitor	% Non-visitor	Total	Valid weighted N
(Has access ONLY to cells)	74.5%	25.5%	100.0%	19
Almost always on a cell phone	42.3%	57.7%	100.0%	803
Usually on a cell phone	54.5%	45.5%	100.0%	394
(On a cell about HALF)	44.0%	56.0%	100.0%	23
Sometimes on a cell phone	51.0%	49.0%	100.0%	918
Almost never on a cell phone	42.1%	57.9%	100.0%	428
(Has NO access to a cell)	26.5%	73.5%	100.0%	95

Chi-square test: $p < .001$

[Note to the reader: When cross-tabulating demographic variables against visitor status, as in Table D1b.2, following statistical convention the percentages total 100 within each row rather than down the columns.]

Table D1b.3. Cross-tabulation by Region (weighted regional data, general public)

Response	AKR	PWR	IMR	MWR	SER	NER	NCR
(Has access ONLY to cells)	0.1%	0.8%	0.6%	1.0%	1.1%	0.4%	--
Almost always on a cell phone	12.0%	23.2%	30.4%	27.2%	30.7%	20.9%	20.8%
Usually on a cell phone	14.8%	17.0%	13.4%	12.7%	10.4%	12.2%	16.0%
(On a cell about HALF)	1.3%	0.5%	1.4%	1.1%	0.1%	0.4%	0.1%
Sometimes on a cell phone	31.9%	27.8%	25.6%	27.3%	28.2%	28.2%	30.9%
Almost never on a cell phone	30.8%	25.0%	23.2%	25.1%	24.4%	29.7%	25.8%
(Has NO access to a cell)	9.1%	5.8%	5.5%	5.7%	5.2%	8.2%	6.4%
Total	100.0%	100.0%	100.0%	100.0%	100.0%	100.0%	100.0%
Valid weighted N	357	370	414	461	388	422	280

Chi-square test: p<.001

D1c. **This question is about the residential phones in your household, not counting cell phones, business lines, or numbers that are only used for a computer or a fax. Including the phone number that we're talking on right now, how many different residential phone numbers ring into this household and can be answered by a person?**

(As needed: A voice-over-Internet phone, on computer, is considered a residential phone. However, if it has the same phone number as another phone in the household, please count that phone number only once. Extension phones that all ring on the same number count as one phone. Don't count cell phones, numbers only used for business, or numbers that can only be answered by a machine.)

Table D1c.1. Frequency Distribution (national data, general public)

Response	Unweighted Frequency	Unweighted Percent	Weighted Percent
0 phones	390	9.6%	20.0%
1 phone	3,062	75.5%	70.4%
2 phones	388	9.6%	6.5%
3 phones	131	3.2%	2.0%
4 phones	44	1.1%	0.7%
5 phones	22	0.5%	0.2%
6 phones	3	0.1%	0.0%
7 or more phones	14	0.3%	0.2%
Total valid	4,054	100.0%	100.0%
(Don't know/Not sure)	12		
(No answer/Refused)	37		
Total missing	49		
Total N	4,103	4,054	2,677

Table D1c.2. Cross-tabulation by Visitation (weighted national data, general public)

Response	% Visitor	% Non-visitor	Total	Valid weighted N
0 phones	43.9%	56.1%	100.0%	534
1 phone	47.7%	52.3%	100.0%	1,886
2 phones	48.2%	51.8%	100.0%	174
3 phones	47.3%	52.7%	100.0%	53
4 phones	47.1%	52.9%	100.0%	17
5 phones	49.0%	51.0%	100.0%	6
6 phones	67.9%	32.1%	100.0%	0.2
7 or more phones	10.3%	89.7%	100.0%	7

Chi-square test: p>.2

Table D1c.3. Cross-tabulation by Region (weighted regional data, general public)

Response	AKR	PWR	IMR	MWR	SER	NER	NCR
0 phones	1.6%	17.6%	24.3%	20.0%	22.8%	13.5%	2.7%
1 phone	93.8%	74.9%	67.1%	72.0%	67.6%	75.7%	85.2%
2 phones	3.6%	6.0%	7.2%	4.5%	6.6%	7.1%	9.0%
3 phones	0.8%	0.8%	1.2%	1.9%	2.4%	2.2%	2.3%
4 phones	0.0%	0.5%	0.1%	1.3%	0.2%	0.7%	0.3%
5 phones	0.1%	0.1%	0.1%	0.3%	0.1%	0.2%	0.2%
6 phones	--	0.0%	--	--	--	0.0%	0.0%
7 or more phones	0.0%	0.1%	0.0%	0.1%	0.3%	0.5%	0.1%
Total	100.0%	100.0%	100.0%	100.0%	100.0%	100.0%	100.0%
Valid weighted N	358	370	415	460	385	416	276

Chi-square test: p<.001

D2. **What is the highest grade of school or year of college that you have completed?**

Table D2.1. Frequency Distribution (national data, general public)

Response	Unweighted Frequency	Unweighted Percent	Weighted Percent
Up to 8th grade	59	1.5%	1.9%
9th to 11th grade	121	3.0%	3.7%
High school graduate or GED certificate	775	19.1%	19.5%
Some college, no degree	885	21.8%	24.4%
Degree from technical school or community college	261	6.4%	7.2%
University degree-BA/BS	971	23.9%	23.8%
Some graduate school, no advanced degree	139	3.4%	3.0%
Graduate degree-MA/MS/JD/MD/PhD, etc.	846	20.9%	16.4%
Total valid	4,057	100.0%	100.0%
(Don't know/Not sure)	8		
(No answer/Refused)	38		
Total missing	46		
Total N	4,103	4,057	2,684

Table D2.2. Cross-tabulation by Visitation (weighted national data, general public)

Response	% Visitor	% Non-visitor	Total	Valid weighted N
Up to 8th grade	7.4%	92.6%	100.0%	52
9th to 11th grade	21.0%	79.0%	100.0%	100
High school graduate or GED	30.7%	69.3%	100.0%	524
Some college, no degree	47.3%	52.7%	100.0%	655
Degree from technical school or community college	46.7%	53.3%	100.0%	193
University degree-BA/BS	54.1%	45.9%	100.0%	638
Some graduate school, no advanced degree	54.2%	45.8%	100.0%	81
Graduate degree-MA/MS/JD/MD/PhD, etc.	63.0%	37.0%	100.0%	439

Chi-square test: p<.001

Table D2.3. Cross-tabulation by Region (weighted regional data, general public)

Response	AKR	PWR	IMR	MWR	SER	NER	NCR
Up to 8th grade	1.7%	3.9%	1.8%	0.9%	3.6%	1.6%	2.2%
9th to 11th grade	1.4%	4.3%	4.0%	4.7%	5.4%	2.5%	2.6%
High school graduate or GED	22.6%	17.8%	22.1%	20.0%	21.0%	22.3%	18.9%
Some college, no degree	28.2%	26.0%	25.0%	24.0%	25.5%	20.5%	12.0%
Degree from technical school or community college	5.7%	6.1%	5.7%	8.4%	7.2%	8.1%	4.9%
University degree-BA/BS	22.6%	23.9%	23.8%	24.7%	20.0%	23.2%	24.4%
Some graduate school, no advanced degree	4.3%	2.5%	2.7%	3.0%	2.0%	4.3%	3.9%
Graduate degree-MA/MS/JD/MD/PhD, etc.	13.4%	15.5%	15.0%	14.3%	15.3%	17.5%	31.1%
Total	100.0%	100.0%	100.0%	100.0%	100.0%	100.0%	100.0%
Valid weighted N	354	372	416	460	386	423	275

Chi-square test: p<.001

D3. **Are you single, married, living with a life partner, divorced, separated, or widowed?**

Table D3.1. Frequency Distribution (national data, general public)

Response	Unweighted Frequency	Unweighted Percent	Weighted Percent
Single	865	21.4%	24.5%
Married	2,131	52.8%	56.1%
Living with a life partner	196	4.9%	4.9%
Divorced	457	11.3%	8.5%
Separated	62	1.5%	1.2%
Widowed	322	8.0%	4.7%
Total valid	4,033	100.0%	100.0%
(Don't know/Not sure)	10		
(No answer/Refused)	60		
Total missing	70		
Total N	4,103	4,033	2,675

Table D3.2. Cross-tabulation by Visitation (weighted national data, general public)

Response	% Visitor	% Non-visitor	Total	Valid weighted N
Single	37.3%	62.7%	100.0%	656
Married	52.1%	47.9%	100.0%	1,502
Living with a life partner	51.3%	48.7%	100.0%	130
Divorced	42.0%	58.0%	100.0%	228
Separated	48.2%	51.8%	100.0%	33
Widowed	32.0%	68.0%	100.0%	127

Chi-square test: p<.001

Table D3.3. Cross-tabulation by Region (weighted regional data, general public)

Response	AKR	PWR	IMR	MWR	SER	NER	NCR
Single	16.9%	24.2%	26.8%	21.9%	24.0%	26.3%	44.0%
Married	62.7%	54.4%	52.0%	59.7%	54.1%	55.8%	31.1%
Living with a life partner	6.0%	6.9%	6.7%	4.4%	5.0%	3.8%	7.4%
Divorced	9.4%	8.2%	8.1%	7.5%	9.7%	8.1%	8.4%
Separated	1.2%	1.6%	2.2%	0.2%	1.4%	1.1%	2.6%
Widowed	3.7%	4.6%	4.2%	6.3%	5.8%	4.9%	6.5%
Total	100.0%	100.0%	100.0%	100.0%	100.0%	100.0%	100.0%
Valid weighted N	353	370	417	456	387	419	274

Chi-square test: p<.001

D4. **Are you Hispanic or Latino** [Latina]**?**

Table D4.1. Frequency Distribution (national data, general public)

Response	Unweighted Frequency	Unweighted Percent	Weighted Percent
Yes (Hispanic)	289	7.1%	13.0%
No	3,756	92.9%	87.0%
Total valid	4,045	100.0%	100.0%
(Don't know/Not sure)	9		
(No answer/Refused)	49		
Total missing	58		
Total N	4,103	4,045	2,679

Table D4.2. Cross-tabulation by Visitation (weighted national data, general public)

Response	% Visitor	% Non-visitor	Total	Valid weighted N
Yes (Hispanic)	32.2%	67.8%	100.0%	348
No	48.6%	51.4%	100.0%	2,331

Chi-square test: p<.001

Table D4.3. Cross-tabulation by Region (weighted regional data, general public)

Response	AKR	PWR	IMR	MWR	SER	NER	NCR
Yes (Hispanic)	4.7%	25.1%	25.9%	5.7%	12.7%	10.1%	8.8%
No	95.3%	74.9%	74.1%	94.3%	87.3%	89.9%	91.2%
Total	100.0%	100.0%	100.0%	100.0%	100.0%	100.0%	100.0%
Valid weighted N	356	372	417	458	388	421	276

Chi-square test: p<.001

D5. **I'm going to read a list of racial categories. Please select one or more to describe your race. Are you ...**

(Read choices one at a time, and mark ALL that apply.)

Table D5.1. Multiple Response Frequencies (national data, general public)

Response	Unweighted Frequency	Unweighted Percent	Weighted Percent
American Indian or Alaska Native	216	5.6%	3.5%
Asian	94	2.4%	3.9%
Black or African American	400	10.4%	13.2%
Native Hawaiian or other Pacific Islander	29	0.8%	1.0%
White	3,270	85.1%	80.8%
(Don't know/Not sure)	101		
(No answer/Refused)	158		
Total missing	259		
Total N	4,103	3,844	2,469

This is a mark-all-that-apply question; percentages total more than 100.

Table D5.2. Frequency Distribution for Race/Ethnicity (recoded national data, general public)

Response	Unweighted Frequency	Unweighted Percent	Weighted Percent
Hispanic, any race	289	7.3%	13.2%
White only, non-Hispanic	3,017	76.0%	68.5%
Black only, non-Hispanic	359	9.0%	11.7%
Other only, non-Hispanic	169	4.3%	5.1%
Two or more, non-Hispanic	137	3.5%	1.5%
Total valid	3,971	100.0%	100.0%
(Don't know/Not sure)	28		
(No answer/Refused)	104		
Total missing	132		
Total N	4,103	3,971	2,636

Table D5.3. Race/Ethnicity by Visitation (weighted national data, general public)

Response	% Visitor	% Non-visitor	Total	Valid weighted N
Hispanic, any race	32.2%	67.8%	100.0%	348
White only, non-Hispanic	52.6%	47.4%	100.0%	1,807
Black only, non-Hispanic	28.0%	72.0%	100.0%	307
Other only, non-Hispanic	47.7%	52.3%	100.0%	135
Two or more, non-Hispanic	31.5%	68.5%	100.0%	39

Chi-square test: $p < .001$

Table D5.4. Race/Ethnicity by Region (weighted regional data, general public)

Response	AKR	PWR	IMR	MWR	SER	NE	DC
Hispanic, any race	4.7%	26.0%	26.2%	5.8%	12.9%	10.3%	9.1%
White only, non-Hispanic	65.3%	50.3%	55.8%	78.4%	62.9%	68.6%	35.1%
Black only, non-Hispanic	1.1%	6.3%	7.3%	7.6%	14.5%	8.3%	49.0%
Other only, non-Hispanic	20.0%	11.6%	5.2%	4.8%	4.3%	7.0%	3.0%
Two or more, non-Hispanic	8.9%	5.9%	5.5%	3.4%	5.4%	5.9%	3.8%
Total	100.0%	100.0%	100.0%	100.0%	100.0%	100.0%	100.0%
Valid weighted N	356	360	412	450	382	413	267

Chi-square test: $p < .001$

[Note to the reader: Table D5.2 combines the Hispanic "ethnicity" data from Question D4 with the "race" data from Question D5, producing mutually exclusive race/ethnicity categories for use in Tables D5.3 and D5.4.

Because of small cell sizes, the "other only, non-Hispanic" group combines into a single category all non-Hispanics who selected as their racial group only Asian, American Indian/Alaska Native, or Native Hawaiian/Other Pacific Islander. Similarly, the "two or more, non-Hispanic" category includes those non-Hispanics who self-identified as being in any two racial groups or more.]

D6. **In what year were you born?**

Table D6.1. Frequency Distribution (recoded national data, general public)

Response	Unweighted Frequency	Unweighted Percent	Weighted Percent
18-24 years old	238	6.0%	12.5%
25-44 years old	1,099	27.9%	36.1%
45-64 years old	1,757	44.6%	34.5%
65 or older	847	21.5%	16.9%
Total valid	3,941	100.0%	100.0%
(Don't know/Not sure)	7		
(No answer/Refused)	155		
Total missing	162		
Total N	4,103	3,941	2,601

Table D6.2. Cross-tabulation by Visitation (weighted national data, general public)

Response	% Visitor	% Non-visitor	Total	Valid weighted N
18-24 years old	35.0%	65.0%	100.0%	325
25-44 years old	48.5%	51.5%	100.0%	939
45-64 years old	53.0%	47.0%	100.0%	898
65 or older	40.0%	60.0%	100.0%	439

Chi-square test: $p<.001$

Table D6.3. Cross-tabulation by Region (weighted regional data, general public)

Response	AKR	PWR	IMR	MWR	SER	NER	NCR
18-24 years old	11.0%	12.9%	13.7%	12.6%	12.3%	12.5%	9.9%
25-44 years old	40.7%	38.1%	38.6%	35.2%	34.7%	34.8%	43.3%
45-64 years old	37.8%	33.4%	32.6%	34.8%	34.6%	35.0%	31.4%
65 or older	10.5%	15.6%	15.1%	17.4%	18.4%	17.7%	15.4%
Total	100.0%	100.0%	100.0%	100.0%	100.0%	100.0%	100.0%
Valid weighted N	349	365	403	446	381	406	264

Chi-square test: $p>.2$

D7. Does anyone in your household have a disability or impairment that could cause them to face problems with access or services during a visit to a unit of the National Park System?

Table D7.1. Frequency Distribution (national data, general public)

Response	Unweighted Frequency	Unweighted Percent	Weighted Percent
Yes (disability)	645	15.9%	14.3%
No	3,421	84.1%	85.7%
Total valid	4,066	100.0%	100.0%
(Don't know/Not sure)	6		
(No answer/Refused)	31		
Total missing	37		
Total N	4,103	4,066	2,689

Table D7.2. Cross-tabulation by Visitation (weighted national data, general public)

Response	% Visitor	% Non-visitor	Total	Valid weighted N
Yes (disability)	42.3%	57.7%	100.0%	383
No	47.2%	52.8%	100.0%	2,306

Chi-square test: p=.076

Table D7.3. Cross-tabulation by Region (weighted regional data, general public)

Response	AKR	PWR	IMR	MWR	SER	NER	NCR
Yes (disability)	13.8%	16.3%	17.2%	14.9%	14.5%	14.7%	9.5%
No	86.2%	83.7%	82.8%	85.1%	85.5%	85.3%	90.5%
Total	100.0%	100.0%	100.0%	100.0%	100.0%	100.0%	100.0%
Valid weighted N	357	373	420	462	388	422	277

Chi-square test: p=.168

D8. [If Yes to item D7] What kind of disability or impairment?

(As needed, read choices. Note: "Sustained" means 6 months or more. Check all that respondent reports.)

Table D8.1. Multiple Response Frequencies (national data, general public with disability in the household)

Response	Unweighted Frequency	Unweighted Percent	Weighted Percent
Blindness, severe vision impairment	31	4.9%	5.2%
Deafness, severe hearing impairment	26	4.1%	5.2%
Substantial limits on walking/climbing/reaching/lifting/carrying	455	72.1%	68.3%
Mental - sustained difficulty learning/remembering/concentrating	56	8.9%	9.4%
(Any other condition that cannot be coded above)	122	19.3%	20.5%
(Don't know/Not sure)	3		
(No answer/Refused)	11		
No disability	3,458		
Total missing	3,472		
Total N	4,103	631	375

This is a mark-all-that-apply question; percentages total more than 100.

D9. How many children under the age of 18 currently live in your household?

Table D9.1. Frequency Distribution (national data, general public)

Response	Unweighted Frequency	Unweighted Percent	Weighted Percent
0 children	2,778	68.6%	61.5%
1 child	550	13.6%	17.1%
2 children	475	11.7%	14.2%
3 children	168	4.1%	4.6%
4 children	59	1.5%	2.0%
5 children	15	0.4%	0.4%
6 children	5	0.1%	0.1%
7 children	2	0.0%	0.0%
Total valid	4,052	100.0%	100.0%
(Don't know/Not sure)	2		
(No answer/Refused)	49		
Total missing	51		
Total N	4,103	4,052	2,670

Table D9.2. Cross-tabulation by Visitation (weighted national data, general public)

Response	% Visitor	% Non-visitor	Total	Valid weighted N
0 children	46.7%	53.3%	100.0%	1,641
1 child	47.7%	52.3%	100.0%	457
2 children	46.9%	53.1%	100.0%	380
3 children	39.9%	60.1%	100.0%	123
4 children	44.0%	56.0%	100.0%	54
5 children	54.9%	45.1%	100.0%	9
6 children	22.2%	77.8%	100.0%	4
7 children	100.0%	--	100.0%	1

Chi-square test: p>.2

Table D9.3. Cross-tabulation by Region (weighted regional data, general public)

Response	AKR	PWR	IMR	MWR	SER	NER	NCR
0 children	49.2%	59.9%	60.7%	60.5%	65.4%	63.8%	68.3%
1 child	19.8%	14.1%	16.0%	18.7%	16.1%	18.0%	12.9%
2 children	20.4%	15.0%	14.5%	14.4%	13.9%	12.0%	13.2%
3 children	7.5%	6.4%	5.4%	4.3%	1.7%	5.1%	4.3%
4 children	2.2%	4.1%	2.4%	1.4%	1.9%	1.0%	0.7%
5 children	0.3%	--	0.8%	0.6%	1.0%	--	0.6%
6 children	0.3%	0.5%	0.2%	--	--	0.1%	--
7 children	0.3%	--	--	0.2%	--	--	--
Total	100.0%	100.0%	100.0%	100.0%	100.0%	100.0%	100.0%
Valid weighted N	356	373	413	457	384	422	280

Chi-square test: p<.01

D9a. [If One or more on item Q9] **How much do you agree or disagree with this statement: "My children are not interested in visiting National Park System units."**

(As needed: Would you say you "strongly agree," "somewhat agree," "neither agree nor disagree," "somewhat disagree," or "strongly disagree" with this statement?)

Table D9a.1. Frequency Distribution (national data, general public with children in the household)

Response	Unweighted Frequency	Unweighted Percent	Weighted Percent
Strongly agree	78	6.4%	7.7%
Somewhat agree	84	6.8%	7.3%
Neither agree nor disagree	71	5.8%	5.4%
Somewhat disagree	184	15.0%	16.9%
Strongly disagree	810	66.0%	62.8%
Total valid	1,227	100.0%	100.0%
(Don't know/Not sure)	42		
(No answer/Refused)	5		
No children	2,829		
Total missing	2,876		
Total N	4,103	1,227	992

Table D9a.2. Cross-tabulation by Visitation (weighted regional data, recent visitors/non-visitors with children in the household)

Response	Visitor	Non-visitor
Strongly agree	4.6%	10.4%
Somewhat agree	6.9%	7.6%
Neither agree nor disagree	4.6%	6.0%
Somewhat disagree	14.1%	19.3%
Strongly disagree	69.9%	56.7%
Total	100.0%	100.0%
Valid weighted N	463	528

Chi-square test: p<.001

D10. Which one of the following income groups best describes your total household income in [previous year], before taxes? Please stop me when I read the correct category.

Table D10.1. Frequency Distribution (national data, general public)

Response	Unweighted Frequency	Unweighted Percent	Weighted Percent
Less than $10,000	179	5.1%	5.7%
$10,000 to $25,000	394	11.3%	12.0%
$25,000 to $50,000	804	23.1%	23.0%
$50,000 to $75,000	735	21.1%	22.8%
$75,000 to $100,000	520	14.9%	13.8%
$100,000 to $150,000	478	13.7%	13.5%
Over $150,000	369	10.6%	9.2%
Total valid	3,479	100.0%	100.0%
(Don't know/Not sure)	143		
(No answer/Refused)	481		
Total missing	624		
Total N	4,103	3,479	2,289

Table D10.2. Cross-tabulation by Visitation (weighted national data, general public)

Response	% Visitor	% Non-visitor	Total	Valid weighted N
Less than $10,000	21.5%	78.5%	100.0%	131
$10,000 to $25,000	36.1%	63.9%	100.0%	274
$25,000 to $50,000	41.7%	58.3%	100.0%	527
$50,000 to $75,000	47.8%	52.2%	100.0%	523
$75,000 to $100,000	58.5%	41.5%	100.0%	316
$100,000 to $150,000	63.4%	36.6%	100.0%	309
Over $150,000	68.5%	31.5%	100.0%	209

Chi-square test: $p < .001$

Table D10.3. Cross-tabulation by Region (weighted regional data, general public)

Response	AKR	PWR	IMR	MWR	SER	NER	NCR
Less than $10,000	3.9%	5.5%	5.7%	8.2%	6.9%	4.6%	4.3%
$10,000 to $25,000	8.0%	14.2%	16.3%	11.1%	15.7%	10.3%	10.5%
$25,000 to $50,000	18.0%	21.1%	26.2%	24.6%	28.5%	20.3%	27.2%
$50,000 to $75,000	22.7%	19.3%	18.6%	23.4%	20.1%	28.3%	16.5%
$75,000 to $100,000	20.2%	11.9%	13.3%	14.8%	12.3%	14.6%	11.6%
$100,000 to $150,000	17.9%	14.4%	14.2%	10.3%	9.0%	14.7%	14.5%
Over $150,000	9.3%	13.6%	5.7%	7.5%	7.5%	7.3%	15.6%
Total	100.0%	100.0%	100.0%	100.0%	100.0%	100.0%	100.0%
Valid weighted N	321	318	350	398	333	349	236

Chi-square test: $p < .001$

D11. (Respondent's gender; code without asking, unless unclear. As needed: And I'm required to ask, are you male or female?)

Table D11.1. Frequency Distribution (national data, general public)

Response	Unweighted Frequency	Unweighted Percent	Weighted Percent
Male	1,909	46.6%	48.5%
Female	2,188	53.4%	51.5%
Total valid	4,097	100.0%	100.0%
(Not coded)	6		
Total N	4,103	4,097	2,702

Table D11.2. Cross-tabulation by Visitation (weighted national data, general public)

Response	% Visitor	% Non-visitor	Total	Valid weighted N
Male	49.3%	50.7%	100.0%	1,310
Female	44.0%	56.0%	100.0%	1,392

Chi-square test: p<.01

Table D11.3. Cross-tabulation by Region (weighted regional data, general public)

Response	AKR	PWR	IMR	MWR	SER	NER	NCR
Male	51.1%	49.6%	49.6%	48.5%	48.2%	48.0%	45.0%
Female	48.9%	50.4%	50.4%	51.5%	51.8%	52.0%	55.0%
Total	100.0%	100.0%	100.0%	100.0%	100.0%	100.0%	100.0%
Valid weighted N	362	375	422	465	389	425	284

Chi-square test: p>.2

D12. That concludes the survey. Thank you very much for participating! Do you have any questions for me?

Literature Cited

Brick, J. Michael, W. Sherman Edwards, and Sunghee Lee. 2007. "Sampling Telephone Numbers and Adults, Interview Length, and Weighting in the California Health Interview Survey Cell Phone Pilot Study." Public Opinion Quarterly, Vol. 71, Issue 5: 793-813.

Dorofeev, Sergey and Peter Grant. 2006. *Statistics for Real Life Sample Surveys: Non-simple-random Samples and Weighted Data*. London: Cambridge University Press.

Grandjean, Burke D., Martha Leighty, Patricia A. Taylor, and Ying Xu. 2004. "Is Target Selection by Last Birthday 'Random Enough'? A Split-Ballot Test." Proceedings of the Annual Meeting of the American Association for Public Opinion Research, May 14, 2004, Miami, Florida.

Keeter, Scott, Courtney Kennedy, April Clark, Trevor Thompson, and Mike Mokrzycki. 2007. "What's Missing from National RDD Surveys? The Impact of the Growing Cell-Only Population." Paper presented at the American Association for Public Opinion Research, May 17-20, 2007. Orange County, California.

National Park Service. 2001. "National Park Service Comprehensive Report of the American Public: Technical Report 2001." Retrieved at: http://www.nature.nps.gov/socialscience/products.cfm#Comprehensive_Survey.

Willis, Gordon B. 2005. *Cognitive Interviewing: A Tool for Improving Questionnaire Design*. Thousand Oaks, California: Sage Publications.

NPS 999/106556, August 2011